DIANE SEED'S ROME FOR ALL SEASONS

A COOKBOOK

DIANE SEED'S ROME
FOR ALL SEASONS
A COOKBOOK

Diane Seed

Illustrated by
Marlene McLoughlin

TEN SPEED PRESS
Berkeley, California

To the memory of Cleo, "a lass unparalleled."

Diane Seed runs a cooking school in her home in Rome:
E-mail 100525.1613@Compuserve.com

A Kirsty Melville book

Ten Speed Press
P.O. Box 7123
Berkeley, CA 94707

Distributed in Australia by E.J. Dwyer Pty Ltd; in Canada by Publishers Group West;
in New Zealand by Tandem Press; and in South Africa by Real Books.

Text and cover design by Nancy Austin
Printed in Hong Kong

Library of Congress Cataloging-in-Publication Data
Seed, Diane.
        Diane Seed's Rome for all seasons: a cookbook/ by Diane Seed;
    illustrated by Marlene McLoughlin.
            p. cm.
        Includes index.
        ISBN 0-89815-849-4
        1. Cookery, Italian. 2. Cookery–Italy–Rome. I. Title.
    TX723.S374 1996
    641.5945–dc20
                                                    96–14059
                                                    CIP

1 2 3 4 5 6 7 8 9 10 — 99 98 97 96

CONTENTS

INTRODUCTION

I have lived, cooked, and eaten in Rome for over twenty-five years, but I have never lost the sense of wonder and excitement at the beginning of every season as the fresh new produce appears in the local markets.

I am sitting here in August in a seemingly empty city that shimmers all day in a heat haze that is almost a bodily assault. The city comes to life in the cooler perfumed evening when a slight breeze whispers through the piazzas, and the whole population takes to the streets, turning them into a vast open-air living room. Since living and eating are synonymous in Rome, the sidewalks are festooned with tables and chairs where you can enjoy an *aperitivo* or gelato. The serious business of eating comes much later, and in the summer it is quite usual to dine at 10 or 11 PM. To ensure no hunger pang goes unsatisfied, the stalls selling great piles of melons stay open all night, and it is always possible to round off the night with a visit to the baker's shop to sample the hot *cornetti* being baked for the following morning's breakfast.

Yet even as I write this I am already thinking that very soon October will be here, and the *bei ottobrini Romani*—the beautiful October days—will bring forth glistening chestnuts, grotesque but succulent *funghi porcini*, tasty artichokes, cardoons, and pumpkins. Pork and lamb return to the butcher's shop, and winter brings the great soups made with dry beans, lentils, and root vegetables. Those of us with fireplaces replenish the woodpile, and look forward to meat grilled with fresh herbs, and toasted coarse bread anointed with olive oil and garlic.

By the end of February, we are getting a little restless and waiting for the first small sweet peas, *fave*, and zucchini. The spring artichokes and asparagus are next on the scene, and the berries inspire new desserts while we wait for the apricots and peaches.

I find it impossible to say which is my favorite season. The important thing is that food in Italy is still seasonal, so every new season seems like a Christmas morning with a stocking full of presents waiting to be unwrapped.

These recipes are chosen from the selection of dishes I enjoy cooking in Rome. Many of them are traditional Roman dishes, dating back to classical times, some have been adopted from other regions of Italy, and others have been created by lightening Rome's culinary heritage. Inevitably, I have had to omit some favorites to keep a balanced selection, and to avoid seeming to ape Pope Clement VII, of whom it was said:

> The Pope does nothing but eat,
>
> The Pope does nothing but sleep.

I would like to thank my family and all my friends who share my meals, for in the words of the Roman proverb, *Chi magna da solo se strozza* (who eats alone chokes).

Historical Background

The Roman soldiers lived on bread, pulses, and garlic in huge quantities, to give some savor to this rather Spartan diet. The legions marched from Rome with these basic field rations, giving rise to the saying, *Ubi Roma ibi allium* (where there are Romans there's garlic). They supplemented this diet with vegetables, eggs, and the occasional chicken "liberated" on their marches. The poor citizens did not fare much better, and Plutarch said the smell of onions and garlic was the smell of poverty, a sentiment shared by many young European dandies doing the Grand Tour in the eighteenth century. More fortunate Roman citizens enjoyed eggs, cheese, and honey, and from the Etruscans Rome learned to make wine and olive oil. Dormice, snails, and small birds enriched the daily fare, and in the days of the Republic laws existed to curb extravagant meals. An edict of 161 BC prohibited artificial livestock fattening, and limited the consumption of chickens to one per day.

The Empire ushered in a reign of hedonism, and Petronius describes many "over the top" banquets. Even venerable patricians ate well, and the great estates were stocked with wild animals and game. Originally the *leporaria* were established to breed hare, which were considered a great delicacy, but eventually deer and wild boar were kept behind the high walls of thirty-acre *leporaria*. The extensive empire was plundered to bring back to Rome exotic edible feasts, but oxen and cows could not be slaughtered, since oxen were needed to work in the fields and cows to provide milk. Transgressors risked exile or death.

Roman culture disappeared with the barbarian invasions from the north, but by the Middle Ages lambs and pigs from the neighboring countryside were entering Rome on hoof and grazing in the ruined Colosseum before being slaughtered. The Church calendar influenced eating habits with its compulsory "lean" days, and *osterie* and trattorias sprang up to feed and house the growing troops of pilgrims. During papal elections the city was thronged with emissaries from foreign rulers, and these in turn attracted bands of courtesans, mountebanks, and merchants that all had to be fed. The Sabine hills to the north, the Pontine marshes, and the pastoral Ciociaria to the south helped fill the larders, and wine arrived in sixty-liter loads by cart from the Castelli Romani, the small wine-producing hill towns south of Rome. In the sixteenth century Pope Pius V decided to tax the meat and table wine coming into Rome, and the income produced was enough to pay the yearly repairs to the Sisto Bridge and the bridge to and from the island in the Tiber. Many of the popes and cardinals were notorious gluttons, employing an army of cooks. The papal elections were speeded up by limiting the food served to the conclave. After three days the cardinals were fed only one course, and after five days they were reduced to bread and water.

With the Crusades and the trading of the great marine republics, Genoa, Pisa, Venice, and Amalfi, new ingredients came into Italian cooking: artichokes, eggplants (aubergines), spinach, citrus fruits, and sugar. All roads led to Rome, and these foods soon arrived at the city, which bartered salt from the Pontine marshes in exchange for new ingredients. Yet the Romans remained faithful to traditional dishes and continued to prize cereal, pulses, and homely vegetables. With the discovery of the New World, tomatoes, sweet peppers (capsicums), corn, and beans found their way to Roman kitchens, and the city learned to adapt traditional recipes to include these new tastes.

When in 1870 Rome became the capital of the new Italian nation, a massive building program was started to provide suitably grandiose edifices to house the different ministries and foreign embassies. The private gardens were swallowed up, and as the city started to spread, fewer families were able to keep chickens and pigs, or grow their own vegetables. More trattorias were needed to feed the visitors, and since Italian cooking was still fiercely regional, different menus were offered according to the cook's birthplace. Even twenty years ago trattorias still boasted "Cucina Emiliana" or "Cucina Veneta" beside, or instead of, their name. When Italy was united the ghetto was opened up, and Roman cooking was enriched by the influx of traditional Orthodox Jewish recipes. The Jews had been confined here since the sixteenth century, and a large proportion of Roman dishes originated and survived intact, untouched by foreign influence, thanks to the Jewish population.

In the 1950s, Hollywood discovered Rome, and films like *Roman Holiday* and *Three Coins in the Fountain* lured visitors to Rome. *Osterie* became restaurants, and film stars were photographed eating glistening mounds of golden fettuccine at Alfredo's. By the beginning of the sixties, Roman cooking was based on good home cooking, with larger amounts of rich ingredients like eggs and butter. People became more prosperous and the eating habits changed. Women became liberated, and joined the nation's work force outside the home. This meant more money to spend on food, but less time to prepare it. To date, the nation's grandmothers have kept the culinary traditions alive, but convenience food from supermarkets is making frightening inroads. The advent of *nouvelle cuisine* in France caused large ripples in Italy, and people began to be more adventurous, eating dishes from other regions and regarding new ingredients with less suspicion. Today, avocados, gingerroot, and exotic fruit can be bought all over Rome, but these new ingredients have not supplanted old favorites, merely enlarged the shoppers' repertoire.

As in the past, all roads lead to Rome, and today it is possible to buy produce from all over Italy, and often the best produce is shipped directly to Rome, where it can be sold at a more advantageous price. This has inevitably affected Roman cooking, but in a positive way, so new lighter dishes exist side by side with the robust dishes of the past. For today's cook, Roman markets are for all seasons and all regions. The choice is infinite.

Please Note

All the recipes in this book serve 4, except for the pasta recipes, which serve 4 as a first course, 2 as a main course.

DIANE SEED'S ROME FOR ALL SEASONS

A COOKBOOK

PASTA, RICE & SOUPS

Flour-and-water ribbon pasta existed in a rudimentary form in ancient Rome. A coarse unleavened bread made with flour and water was flattened and cooked on the hearth. It was then cut into strips and cooked with cereals, pulses, or vegetables. The pasta was called *laganum* in Latin, and today some recipes still use the term *laganelli*. This tradition of homemade flour-and-water pasta still exists, and in the rural areas outside Rome this humble pasta was dressed up with amusing names like *ceca-maritie* (husband blinders), *strozzapreti* (priest chokers), or *fregnacce* (thinga-majigs).

In more prosperous country areas, eggs were added to make the rich golden fettuccine that today has become one of the glories of Roman cooking. In some of the city convents the nuns produced thin golden *capelli d'angelo* (angel hair), which was bought for special occasions, like the birth of a new baby.

In the sixteenth century the powerful Guild of Vermicelli Makers established itself near the Pantheon, and today Via delle Paste and Via dei Pastini still exist. The first industrial dried durum wheat pasta was made in Naples in the seventeenth century, and by the end of the nineteenth century Romans were enjoying dishes of *maccheroni*, which was the generic name for durum wheat pasta. Today spaghetti, linguine, bucatini, and penne are some of the favorite shapes.

Pasta should be cooked in a large, tall pan, and 1 pound of pasta needs to be cooked in approximately 14 cups water with 2 tablespoons coarse salt. It not only tastes better when it still has some texture, it is also more digestible, so drain it while it is still al dente. Remember the sauce has to wait for the pasta, not the pasta for the sauce, so plan your time carefully, and move quickly when you are putting it all together. In modern Italy pasta is eaten as a first course, so the quantities given will provide 4 people with a generous starter, 2 people a main course.

Rice was introduced into Sicily during the Spanish domination, but geographical conditions did not suit the crop, and it only established itself in Italy when one of the Sforza dukes took some seeds back to Milan and sowed the crop along the River Po. Romans enjoy an occasional risotto with interesting fish or vegetables, but their real passion is reserved for pasta. To make a successful risotto you need a rice that will absorb liquid but stay intact. In order of preference, use Vialone, Carnaroli, or Arborio.

Minestre are the direct descendants of the Roman *puls,* which sustained the legions on their forced marches. They were thick broths made with boiled cereal and pulses, occasionally cooked in milk. Fava beans, lentils, and chick-peas were favorite ingredients, and modern Romans share the same taste, although today's *minestre* are usually thickened by puréeing some of the cooked pulses and adding pasta or rice. By comparison, traditional Roman soups are usually clear, and many of the soups found today have been adopted from other regions.

Linguine alle Mazzancolle
Linguine with Shrimp

I love to cook this recipe in early June, when we come back from the market, laden with food shopping, feeling hot and slightly cross. A glass of white Friuli wine, like Jermann's Sauvignon, begins to work its magic, as the water is put on to boil in the pasta pan, and we struggle to fit all the shopping into the refrigerator and vegetable storage baskets. Over the years my family has gotten smaller and my refrigerators have gotten bigger—I now have a huge American model—but nothing can contain the exuberance of our too lavish shopping. By the second glass of wine, the shrimp (prawns) are cleaned, the kitchen is relatively clear, and we soon sit down to a perfect simple, delicious Roman Saturday lunch.

2 pounds (907 g) large shrimp (prawns), shelled and deveined

2 tablespoons (30 mL) extra virgin olive oil

2 cloves garlic, finely chopped

½-inch (1-cm) square fresh gingerroot, peeled and grated

1 small dried chile pepper

Salt to taste

1 tablespoon (15 mL) fresh lemon juice

1 cup (237 mL) dry white wine

1 pound (454 g) linguine

1 tablespoon chopped fresh parsley

Leave 8 shrimp whole and cut the rest into 2 or 3 large pieces.

In a large pan, heat the oil and gently cook the garlic, gingerroot, and chile pepper. When the garlic begins to change color, add all the shrimp and stir-fry for a few minutes before adding a little salt and the lemon juice. Set aside.

Cook the linguine in a large pot of salted boiling water until not quite al dente; drain. Pour the wine into the shrimp and let it bubble before stirring in the linguine. Cook for 3 minutes while shaking the pan, then add the parsley, stir, and serve.

Linguine ai Peperoni Rossi
Linguine with Red Pepper Sauce

Many of my favorite recipes call for the peppers (capsicums) to be roasted and the skin removed, and although I love the rich, tantalizing smell of roasting peppers, I hate the mess and dirty fingernails caused by the actual skinning, so I tend to cook these recipes in summer when the skin seems to want to come off. This recipe mercifully calls for the cooked peppers to be passed through a food mill, so there is no need to skin them first.

¼ cup (30 mL) extra virgin olive oil

1 onion, chopped

6 large red bell peppers (capsicums), seeded, ribs removed, and coarsely chopped

2 large tomatoes, chopped

Salt to taste

14 ounces (397 g) linguine

¼ cup (28 g) freshly grated Parmesan cheese

In a large pan, heat the oil and gently cook the onion before adding the peppers. Stir-fry in the oil, then add the tomatoes and a little salt. Cover and stew gently until the peppers have almost melted into the oil. Pass through a food mill to remove the skins.

Cook the linguine in a large pot of salted boiling water until al dente, drain, and toss in the Parmesan before stirring in the pepper sauce.

Linguine al Tonno, Limone, e Rughetta
Linguine with Tuna, Lemon, and Arugula

*O*ver the years this has gradually become one of my favorite pasta dishes, and we eat it all through the year. In Rome we can buy small bunches of wild arugula (rocket) that has a pungent flavor, much stronger than cultivated arugula.

3 tablespoons (44 mL) extra virgin olive oil

2 cloves garlic, finely chopped

1 small dried red chile, crushed

7 ounces (198 g) canned tuna in olive oil, drained and flaked

14 ounces (397 g) linguine

1 cup (28 g) wild or cultivated arugula (rocket) leaves, coarsely chopped

Juice of 2 lemons

Salt to taste

In a large pan, heat the oil and gently cook the garlic and chile. As the garlic begins to change color, add the tuna and stir. Keep warm.

Cook the pasta in a large pot of salted boiling water. If using wild arugula, stir into the pasta when it is halfway cooked, or 2 to 3 minutes before it is al dente. If using cultivated arugula, add it when the pasta is al dente. Drain the pasta and arugula and stir it into the tuna mixture. Squeeze over the lemon juice. Using a wooden spoon, lift up and stir pasta and arugula until the tuna is evenly distributed. Add salt if needed. Serve at once.

Pasta con Pomodori Verdi
Spaghetti with Green Tomato Sauce

Maria from Campo dei Fiori market gave me this recipe one day last spring. As she gave me instructions she picked out the herbs and carefully selected the green tomatoes, rejecting several that seemed perfectly green to me. When I prepared the dish it was a great success, and my friends are in turn passing it on to their friends!

1 cup (43 g) fresh herb leaves, including as many of the following herbs as possible: mint, basil, arugula (rocket), chives, parsley, thyme, dill

5 very green tomatoes, coarsely chopped

1 clove garlic, chopped

2 tablespoons (14 g) freshly grated Parmesan cheese

14 ounces (397 g) spaghetti

4 tablespoons (59 mL) extra virgin olive oil

Salt and black pepper to taste

In a blender or food processor, chop the herbs, tomatoes, and garlic. Add the cheese and briefly process.

Cook the pasta in a large pot of salted boiling water until al dente. Just before draining the pasta, pour the oil into the blender or processor and make a smooth sauce. Add salt and black pepper to taste. Drain the pasta and stir in the sauce. Serve at once.

Spaghetti alle Vongole
Spaghetti with Clams

Roman trattorias have taken this dish to their heart, and it is probably on every menu on Fridays, and quite frequently on other days too. The best clam is the vongole verace, *but smaller clams are often substituted. The sauce is so good there is even a "poor," clamless version, with the* vongole *still at sea! Since I am not a lover of clams, I cook that for myself while the others enjoy the complete experience.*

2 pounds (907 g) verace
   clams in the shell,
   scrubbed thoroughly

½ cup (118 mL) water

4 tablespoons (59 mL)
   extra virgin olive oil

2 cloves garlic, chopped

1 small dried chile
   pepper, crushed

½ cup (118 mL) dry white
   wine

14 ounces (397 g)
   spaghetti

2 tablespoons chopped
   fresh parsley

Salt to taste

Place the clams in a pan with the water over high heat and cover until the clams open. Discard any clams that fail to open. Strain the cooking liquid and put to one side.

In a large pan, heat the oil and gently cook the garlic and chile pepper. When the garlic starts to turn color, stir in the clams and pour over their cooking water. Add the wine and simmer for a few minutes. Keep warm.

Cook the pasta in a large pot of lightly salted boiling water until al dente, drain, and stir into the clams. Add the parsley and salt, stir well, and serve.

Spaghetti alla Gricia/Spaghetti alla 'Matriciana
Spaghetti with Garlic, Onion, and Pancetta

This rustic recipe comes from Griciano, in the Sabine hills, not far from the town of Amatrice. Romans took the dish and made it their own, as they did with the Sabine women in ancient times! When a little chopped peeled tomato is added with the garlic and onion, the dish becomes Spaghetti alla 'Matriciana.

3 tablespoons (44 mL)
   olive oil

Small piece dried chile
   pepper

7 ounces (197 g) pancetta
   or bacon

1 small onion, finely
   chopped

2 cloves garlic, finely
   chopped

1 pound (454 g) spaghetti

Salt and black pepper
   to taste

Grated pecorino cheese

2 tomatoes, peeled and
   chopped (see page 119)
   (optional)

In a large pan, gently heat 1 tablespoon (15 mL) of the olive oil, add the chile and pancetta, and let the pancetta fat slowly melt into the oil. Remove the pancetta and add the remaining oil, onion, and garlic. Cook gently until golden brown, discard the chile, return the pancetta to the pan, and keep warm.

Cook the pasta in a large pot of salted boiling water until al dente. Drain and toss in the pecorino before stirring in the onion and tomato mixture (if using). Serve with black pepper.

Spaghettini con Pomodorini Pachino
Spaghettini with Pachino Cherry Tomatoes

In the past, when San Marzano plum tomatoes were not available in winter, everyone in Rome used bottled or canned tomatoes for their pasta sauces. (It is better to use good, full-taste canned tomatoes than insipid-tasting fresh tomatoes.) Then, eating habits were revolutionized by the advent of a small, sweet winter tomato from Pachino in Sicily. They are vine ripened and sold with stalks still intact. The perfume that is released as the stalks are removed signals their very special flavor. This tomato sauce is usually made southern style, without the skins being removed, and the taste is so intense the pasta is usually served without any cheese.

3 tablespoons (44 mL)
   extra virgin olive oil

1 small onion, chopped

1 pound (454 g) small
   full-flavor tomatoes, cut
   into halves

6 leaves basil

Salt and black pepper
   to taste

14 ounces (397 g)
   spaghettini or other
   dried pasta

In a large pan, heat the oil and let the onion soften and begin to change color. Add the tomatoes, and after a few minutes add the basil leaves, salt, and pepper. Cook gently for 15 minutes.

Cook the pasta in a large pot of lightly salted boiling water until al dente. Drain and stir into the tomatoes. Simmer for a few minutes, then serve at once.

Spaghetti con Melanzane, Zucchine, e Orata

Spaghetti with Bream, Eggplant, and Zucchini

I love this combination of fresh fish and vegetables with pasta. I often prepare it for Saturday lunch when we get back from the market. It is a perfect summer one-dish meal.

4 5-ounce (142 g) fillets
of sea bream or porgy,
skinned

Salt and black pepper
to taste

Fish carcass, for stock

2 tablespoons (30 mL)
extra virgin olive oil

1 small onion, chopped

2 small zucchini
(courgettes), sliced

1 eggplant (aubergine),
chopped and left under
salt for 30 minutes
(see page 119)

1 ripe tomato, peeled,
seeded, and cubed
(see page 119)

14 ounces (397 g)
spaghetti

8 leaves basil, coarsely
torn

Season the fish fillets with salt and pepper, cover, and set aside.

To make the stock, wash the fish carcass, place in a stockpot, and cover with water. Add a little salt and boil for 20 minutes. Strain.

In a large pan, heat the oil and gently cook the onion, zucchini, and eggplant for 10 minutes. Stir in the tomato and place the seasoned fish fillets on top. Cover and steam for 5 minutes. Lift the fish fillets out and keep warm. Pour 1 cup (237 mL) of the fish stock into the vegetables, and remove from heat.

Cook the pasta in a large pot of salted boiling water until almost al dente. Drain and stir into the vegetables, adding the basil at the same time. Return to heat and check the seasoning. Lay the fish on top of the vegetables and simmer for a few minutes. Serve at once.

Pasta e Lenticchie
Pasta and Lentils

*T*his dish is cooked to perfection and served with little ceremony by Felice in Via Mastro Giorgio, whose tables are crowded with regulars from Testaccio market. You have to ask with fitting humility if there is a place for you, and Felice sizes you up. If you get a nod, you feel as if St. Peter himself has opened the gates!

1½ cups (300 g) dried green or brown lentils, preferably Castelluccio variety, washed and soaked for several hours

1 small stalk celery, chopped

2 tablespoons (30 mL) extra virgin olive oil, plus extra for garnish (optional)

1 slice pancetta or bacon, chopped

1 small onion, finely chopped

2 cloves garlic, finely chopped

1 small dried chile pepper, crushed

2 red tomatoes, peeled and chopped (see page 119)

Salt to taste

7 ounces (198 g) tubetti, or spaghetti broken into short pieces

1 tablespoon chopped fresh parsley (optional)

Drain the lentils and cook with the celery in 6 cups (1.4 L) boiling water. The exact time needed will depend on the quality of the lentils, and will take from 30 to 90 minutes.

In a large pan, heat the oil and gently melt the fat from the pancetta before adding the onion, garlic, and chile pepper. Stir in the tomatoes and simmer for a few minutes.

When the lentils are cooked, discard the celery, add salt, and throw in the pasta. When the pasta is nearly cooked, stir in the onion mixture and cook together for a few minutes. Stir in the optional parsley, check the seasoning, and serve. Grated pecorino or Parmesan cheese can be handed round separately if desired, but I prefer a fine thread of good extra virgin olive oil drizzled on top, then stirred in.

Pasta e Broccoli in Brodo di Arzilla
Pasta and Broccoli in Skate Sauce

*T*his minestra *used to be served on Church "lean" days, especially Good Friday, or* Venerdi Santo. *As the fast days were abolished, many dishes became almost forgotten, and I had lived in Rome for several years before I came across this dish. In Testaccio market I heard an elderly woman reminiscing about her grandmother's recipe. I decided I must track this most Roman of dishes down. Eventually a 100 percent Roman, not easy to find these days, prepared this version for me. In the past the fish fillets would have been served at another meal, but I place them in individual serving bowls and pour the* minestra *over the top.*

1 small onion, chopped

2 cloves garlic, finely chopped

Salt and black pepper to taste

1 2-pound (907 g) skate, cleaned but left whole

2 tablespoons (30 mL) extra virgin olive oil

1 anchovy fillet, chopped

1 small dried chile pepper, crushed

½ cup (118 mL) dry white wine

3 plum tomatoes, peeled and chopped (see page 119)

10½ ounces (298 g) broccoli florets

7 ounces (198 g) spaghetti, broken into short lengths

1 tablespoon chopped fresh parsley for garnish

In a large pan, bring 5 cups (1.2 L) water to a boil. Add the onion, half the garlic, salt, and pepper. Boil for 10 minutes, then add the whole fish. Lower heat and cook gently for 20 minutes, then lift the fish out carefully so that you do not break it. Remove the fillets and set them to one side. Return the carcass to the pan and cook for another 20 minutes. Strain the stock and keep warm.

In a large pan, heat the oil and gently cook the anchovy, remaining garlic, and chile pepper until soft. Pour on the wine, let it evaporate, then stir in the tomatoes and cook for 15 minutes. Pour over the stock and bring back to a boil. Add the broccoli and cook for another 15 minutes.

Cook the pasta in a large pot of lightly salted boiling water until al dente. Drain and stir into the tomato and broccoli mixture.

Place a little fish in an individual serving bowl, pour the sauce over the top, sprinkle with parsley, and serve.

Fettuccine al Modo Nostro

Fettuccine with Ham, Peas, and Mushrooms

When my daughters were small, this dish, *"fettuccine in our style,"* was a source of constant amusement to them when we went out to eat in local trattorias. It appeared regularly on every menu, and they would take turns asking the waiter, very demurely, what exactly was "their style," and we all had to keep straight faces as the reply was always the same, "ham, peas, and mushrooms." Modo nostro *has been a family favorite ever since. It is particularly good with "straw and hay," or* paglia e fieno, *the mixture of green and yellow pasta.*

1 tablespoon (14 g) butter

3 ½ ounces (99 g) prosciutto, cut into strips

3 ½ ounces (99 g) cultivated mushrooms, cleaned and sliced

1 cup (198 g) shelled peas, cooked lightly in salted water and drained

½ cup (118 mL) heavy (double) cream

18 ounces (510 g) *paglia e fieno* or fettuccine

Salt

4 tablespoons (28 g) freshly grated Parmesan cheese

Black pepper to taste

In a large pan, melt the butter and gently cook the prosciutto and mushrooms until the mushrooms are soft. Stir in the peas, then the cream, and heat gently. Keep warm.

Cook the pasta in a large pot of lightly salted boiling water until al dente, drain, and toss in the Parmesan before stirring into the sauce. Add black pepper to taste, and serve.

Castagne Tagliatelle con Funghi Porcini
Chestnut Tagliatelle with Porcini Mushrooms

Living in Rome, with many good fresh pasta shops close to hand, I only make fresh pasta when I want to use a special pasta dough or a particular filling. In November, I use chestnut flour to make autumn tagliatelle, and I serve them with a sauce of the seasonal porcini mushrooms (cèpes). If you prefer to use dried egg tagliatelle, it will still taste good.

PASTA

2 cups (298 g) chestnut flour

1¼ cups (198 g) all-purpose (plain) flour

5 eggs

Pinch of salt

SAUCE

3 tablespoons (44 mL) extra virgin olive oil

14 ounces (397 g) porcini mushrooms (cèpes), scraped and sponged clean, then sliced

1 clove garlic, chopped finely

1 tablespoon chopped fresh parsley

———

Salt

2 tablespoons (14 g) freshly grated Parmesan (optional)

Black pepper to taste

To make the pasta, combine the chestnut flour and all-purpose flour in a mixing bowl and gradually work in the eggs and salt. Knead well on a lightly floured board or with a heavy-duty mixer fitted with a dough hook. When you have a smooth, elastic dough, cover and keep at room temperature for 15 minutes.

Meanwhile, make the sauce. In a large pan, heat the oil and gently cook the mushrooms and garlic for 10 minutes, stirring frequently. Stir in the parsley, remove from heat, and keep to one side.

Roll out the pasta dough very thinly, using a pasta roller if you have one. Flour the sheets on both sides, roll up, and cut into thin strips. Open out the tagliatelle and arrange in little heaps on a floured board so that they can dry out for about 30 minutes. It will not matter if you leave them several hours. When ready to serve, cook in a large pot of lightly salted boiling water until al dente. Meanwhile, warm the sauce through. Drain the pasta and stir into the warmed sauce. Serve with the cheese handed round separately, and freshly ground pepper.

Tagliolini ai Tartufi Bianchi
Tagliolini with White Truffle

In October, the majestic white truffle comes into its short season, which lasts until the end of the year. It can best be appreciated when served with a neutral base, and when grated lavishly over plain risotto or pasta, it makes a dish fit for the gods or emperors! During the season, I like to eat at Rome's Al Moro, where a huge photograph of the owner's father, in the role of Nero in Fellini's Satyricon, dominates the dining room. I feel it sets the mood for the feast! The price for the truffle is quoted per ten grams, and the waiter brings the truffle to be grated at table. The sublime perfume is irresistible, and lures other diners to similar extravagance. In Rome, during the winter of 1995, white truffles cost U.S. $2,333 per kilogram.

If you do not have a large restaurant-size truffle, I find a truffle shaver is not efficient. I prefer to use a small sharp knife to make fine shavings.

1 fresh white truffle weighing at least 2 ounces (57 g)

14 ounces (397 g) tagliolini

Salt

4 tablespoons (57 g) butter, melted

2 tablespoons (14 g) freshly grated Parmesan cheese

Brush the truffle with a dry brush, scraping if necessary with a sharp vegetable knife to clean it. Cook the pasta in a large pot of salted boiling water until al dente, drain, and toss in melted butter and Parmesan. Serve, grating fine shavings of truffle on top of the pasta when at table.

Timballo di Peperoni
Red Pepper Timbale

*I*n the south of Italy they love to serve sumptuous molded pasta dishes that delight the eye and confound the palate with their rich, intricate fillings. I prefer clean, simple flavors, and over the years I have learned variations that please most people. The great advantage of these baked creations is that unlike most pastas they can be prepared well in advance, and in this recipe the flame-red peppers (capsicums) look sensational.

8 large red bell peppers
  (capsicums), roasted
  and skinned
  (see page 119)

SAUCE

4 tablespoons (59 mL)
  extra virgin olive oil

2 tablespoons (14 g) bread
  crumbs

2 tablespoons pitted and
  chopped (28 g) black
  olives

1 tablespoon (14 g)
  capers, rinsed and
  chopped

1 clove garlic, chopped

2 anchovy fillets, chopped

2 cups (473 mL) fresh
  tomato sauce
  (see page 118)

Divide the roasted peppers into segments and pat dry with paper towels (kitchen paper). Spread out between two layers of paper towels, fold up, and leave for several hours, preferably overnight, so that they become quite dry.

Preheat the oven to 350°F (180°C/gas mark 4).

To make the sauce, heat half the olive oil in a large pan and gently brown the bread crumbs before stirring in the olives, capers, garlic, and anchovies. Add the tomato sauce and warm gently.

MEATBALLS

7 ounces (198 g) ground (minced) lean beef or pork

½ slice bread, soaked in milk, then squeezed out

2 tablespoons (14 g) freshly grated Parmesan cheese

1 tablespoon chopped fresh parsley

1 egg

Basil leaves

Salt and black pepper to taste

———

14 ounces (397 g) penne pasta

1 tablespoon (14 g) fresh ricotta cheese

Olive oil for topping

Basil leaves for garnish

To make the meatballs, put the meat, bread, Parmesan, parsley, egg, basil leaves, and salt and pepper in a food processor. Process to make a smooth paste. Or, mix the ingredients by hand. Form small balls the size of a cherry, and fry lightly in the remaining oil until golden brown.

Cook the pasta in a large pot of lightly salted boiling water until it is pliable but not soft. Drain, and stir in the tomato sauce, ricotta cheese, and meatballs. Line a soufflé dish with non-stick baking parchment, then line with pepper fillets, shiny side facing out. Fill the dish with the pasta and sauce, cover with pepper fillets, a few drops of olive oil, and a circle of baking parchment. (You may not wish to use all pepper fillets; keep surplus for another use.) This can be left to stand at room temperature until ready to complete cooking. Bake for 25 minutes.

Remove from oven and leave to stand for 10 minutes before attempting to turn out. This is most important.

To serve, discard the top paper, cover the top of the soufflé dish with a serving plate, and turn upside down. Remove the dish and peel off the paper. Decorate with basil leaves before taking to the table.

Pennette alla Zucca

Pennette with Pumpkin

Pumpkin is used to make pasta, risotto, gnocchi, and soups, and I was taught how to make the most of this lovely orange vegetable by Angelina Di Mambro, who sells fresh herbs at Ponte Milvio market.

2 tablespoons (30 mL)
   extra virgin olive oil

1 onion, finely chopped

1 clove garlic, finely
   chopped

14 ounces (397 g) peeled
   pumpkin or squash, cut
   into thin sticks

1 cup (237 mL) water

Salt and black pepper
   to taste

1 very small piece dried
   chile pepper, cut into
   thin rings

2 tablespoons chopped
   fresh parsley

14 ounces (397 g) pennette

¼ cup (28 g) freshly
   grated Parmesan cheese

In a large pan, heat the oil and gently cook the onion, garlic, and pumpkin. Add the water, salt, and pepper, then cover and cook gently until the pumpkin is soft, about 10 minutes. Stir in the chile pepper and parsley.

Cook the pasta in a large pot of salted boiling water until al dente, drain, and stir in the Parmesan, then the sauce. Add a little freshly ground black pepper and serve at once.

Zite al Prosciutto

Zite with Prosciutto

This is one of the specialties of the Appia Antica restaurant Cecilia Metella. We have been going there to enjoy eating in their beautiful garden for nearly thirty years, and every time it is difficult to decide whether to start with the baked pasta "scrigno," which I described in my book The Top 100 Pasta Sauces, or the bowl of zite al prosciutto. I have now found the perfect solution. Last Saturday at lunch I started with the zite, and smiling shamelessly, ordered the scrigno for a second course! The zite used at Cecilia Metella measure roughly 4 inches (10 cm). This is a crucial statistic. At that length they are too short to wrap round the fork, and too long to fit neatly into the mouth. It is inevitable that you finish up with a buttery chin, and a feeling of complete immersion. You have to be prepared and avoid wearing silk shirts or snazzy ties, or else tie your table napkin round your neck, ignore the people at the other tables, and enjoy! I suspect those with a beard find the memory lingers on.

4 tablespoons (57 g) butter

7 ounces (198 g) lean prosciutto, chopped

14 ounces (397 g) 4-inch (10-cm) zite

Salt

¾ cup (99 g) freshly grated Parmesan

Black pepper to taste

In a large pan, melt the butter and gently warm the prosciutto.

Cook the pasta in a large pot of lightly salted boiling water until al dente. Drain and stir into the butter and prosciutto. Stir in the cheese and serve. Black pepper should be added to personal taste.

Pasticcio di Maccheroni con Melanzane
Baked Pasta with Eggplant

At the corner of Via del Corso and Piazza Venezia, next to Palazzo Doria, is the house where Madame Letizia Bonaparte used to live. There is a shuttered balcony where she liked to sit unobserved, watching the spectacle of street life. Today I have a similar vantage point from my desk, and my working day is enlivened by chanting protest marches, squealing brakes, police, ambulance, and fire engine sirens, and the raised voices of the mad, the bad, and the happy. In her day the scene was just as noisy, with horse races down the Via del Corso, bands and flamboyant processions for saints' days and Carnival, and elegant carriages sweeping round the square to see and be seen. Madame Bonaparte is said to have had a healthy appetite and to have enjoyed the complicated pasta timballo *prepared for the Roman Carnival. In his* La Grande Cucina, *Luigi Carnacina gives the original recipe, but the combination of sweet pastry casing, lard, giblets, pork, beef, and mushrooms makes it too heavy and time-consuming for modern tastes. This simpler* timballo *belongs to the same tradition, but it is easier on the arteries!*

4 eggplant (aubergines), sliced

Coarse salt for sprinkling

Olive oil for frying

14 ounces (397 g) zite or rigatoni

4 cups (946 mL) fresh tomato sauce (see page 118)

6 leaves basil, torn into small pieces

10½ ounces (298 g) mozzarella, thinly sliced

Freshly grated Parmesan

2 tablespoons (14 g) dried bread crumbs

Sprinkle the eggplant slices with coarse salt and leave for 30 minutes. Rinse well and dry. In a large pan, heat olive oil and fry the eggplant slices in batches until they are golden brown.

Preheat the oven to 400°F (200°C/gas mark 6).

Cook the pasta in a large pot of salted boiling water until it is pliable but not cooked. Drain and toss in the tomato sauce and basil.

Oil a deep ovenproof serving dish and put in a thin layer of pasta. Cover this with a layer of eggplant and a few slices of mozzarella. Sprinkle on some Parmesan and make another layer of pasta. Continue in this way until you have used up all the ingredients, finishing with a layer of eggplant, dotted with small pieces of mozzarella and the bread crumbs mixed with the remaining Parmesan. Bake in the oven for 25 minutes.

Quadrucci e Piselli

Pasta and Peas

In spring, when the small tender peas first appear, they are so good, people want to eat them as often as possible, in as many guises as possible, as long as their delicate flavor is not masked. In Testaccio the older stall holders sit shelling the peas with still nimble fingers, while their children get on with the job of selling. If you are in a hurry, you can buy small bags of already shelled peas, but usually it is a greater pleasure to buy them in the pod, so that you can steal the odd pea as you sit at home companionably shelling them.

2 tablespoons (30 mL) olive oil

1 onion, chopped

½ stalk celery, finely chopped

1 clove garlic

2 slices pancetta or bacon, finely chopped (optional)

10½ ounces (298 g) shelled peas

1 tablespoon chopped fresh parsley

Salt and black pepper to taste

6 cups (1.4 L) light stock (see page 118)

10½ ounces (298 g) fresh or dried egg pasta cut into ½-inch (1cm) squares

6 tablespoons (42 g) freshly grated Parmesan cheese

In a large pan, heat the oil and gently cook the onion, celery, garlic, and pancetta, if used, until soft. Add the peas, parsley, salt, and pepper, and cook gently for 10 minutes. Meanwhile, bring the stock to a boil.

Pour the boiling stock in with the peas. After 3 or 4 minutes, add the pasta. When the pasta is al dente, drain and serve at once with a generous sprinkling of Parmesan over each serving.

Pasta al Pesto

Pasta with Pesto

*A*lthough in Liguria they tell you pesto must be pounded by hand, today very few people have the time, arm muscles, or inclination. Rome has adopted pesto and here very few people even pretend to make it by hand. In spring and summer when basil is in season I make it several times a week, using my food processor to make a delicious sauce in less time than it takes to cook the pasta. I like to leave some rough crumbs of Parmesan and pine nuts to give the sauce some texture. Traditionally in Liguria chestnut pasta was used (see page 16), and some sliced boiled potatoes would be served together with the pasta. Potatoes go beautifully with the pesto sauce.

2 cloves garlic

2 tablespoons pine nuts

¼ cup (28 g) Parmesan cheese, roughly chopped

1 pound (454 g) linguine or spaghetti

1 large bunch basil, stemmed

Salt and black pepper to taste

⅓ cup (78 mL) extra virgin olive oil

In a blender or food processor, purée the garlic, pine nuts, and Parmesan to make a coarse sauce.

Cook the pasta in a large pot of lightly salted boiling water until al dente. Meanwhile, add the basil leaves and the salt and pepper to the mixture in the blender or food processor and process briefly. Just before draining the pasta, add the oil to the food processor and process to make a slightly coarse sauce. Stir the sauce into the pasta, adding 1 tablespoon of pasta water if necessary to coat every strand of pasta with pesto. Serve.

Pasta con Polpettine

Pasta with Meatballs

*T*his is another southern dish that brings instant comfort and gratification. I cook it a lot in the colder months, and I have noticed that people always smile when they eat it. It must be the gastronomic version of "back to the womb."

Traditionally a hard white cheese made with ewe's milk, cacioricotta, is grated over the dish before serving. Pecorino or Parmesan can be used if preferred.

1 slice stale bread,
soaked in milk and then
squeezed out

7 ounces (198 g) minced
lean meat

2 tablespoons (14 g)
freshly grated
Parmesan cheese

1 tablespoon chopped
fresh parsley

Salt and black pepper
to taste

3 cups (710 mL)
fresh tomato sauce
(see page 118)

14 ounces (397 g) bucatini
or another shaped pasta

Cacioricotta, pecorino,
or Parmesan cheese for
grating

In a food processor, combine the bread, meat, Parmesan, parsley, salt, and pepper to make a smooth mixture. Or, mix the ingredients by hand. Form into small meatballs the size of a large cherry, and cook them gently in the tomato sauce for about 15 minutes.

Cook the pasta in a large pot of lightly salted boiling water until al dente. Drain and stir in the sauce. Serve with cheese grated over the top.

Farfalle Verde

Butterfly Pasta with Mint and Green Tomato Sauce

This pasta dish is from Adriana Montellanico's La Briciola restaurant in Grottaferrata. She makes masterly use of the fresh vegetables and herbs from the Castelli Romani, and has adapted many family recipes. Most Italian pasta companies make dried farfalle, but other shaped pasta, like penne, can be used if preferred.

2 tablespoons (30 mL)
   extra virgin olive oil

1 small onion, chopped

1 pound (454 g) green
   tomatoes, peeled and
   chopped (see page 119)

Salt and black pepper
   to taste

¼ cup chopped fresh
   mint, plus a few sprigs
   for garnish

14 ounces (397 g) dried
   farfalle or other shaped
   pasta

2 tablespoons (14 g)
   freshly grated pecorino
   cheese

In a large pan, heat the oil and gently fry the onion until soft. Add the tomatoes, salt, and pepper, and cook for 15 minutes more. Stir in the chopped mint, cook for another 5 minutes, then pass through a food mill.

Cook the pasta in a large pot of lightly salted boiling water until al dente. Drain and stir in the sauce, cheese, and a few sprigs of mint. Serve at once.

Tortelli di Melanzane

Eggplant Tortelli

The Convivio restaurant changes its menu and dishes every day to satisfy the creativity of the young chef, Angelo. This is very praiseworthy, but if you one day discover a superb dish, it is quite likely you will never find it there again. This happened to me with these tortelli, which are stuffed with a small layered melanzane parmigiana *(eggplant [aubergine] Parmesan). Since I cannot count on finding it on the menu ever again, I have experimented and come up with an acceptable copy. Use a pastry cutter if you can only find large eggplant and mozzarella.*

4 thin eggplants (aubergines), 2 inches (5 cm) in diameter, sliced thinly

Coarse salt for sprinkling

Olive oil for frying

Fresh pasta (see page 28)

1 cup (237 mL) fresh tomato sauce (see page 118)

3½ ounces (99 g) mozzarella, sliced into 1¼-inch (3-cm) rounds

7 tablespoons (99 g) butter, melted

¼ cup (28 g) freshly grated Parmesan cheese

8 leaves basil for garnish

Sprinkle the eggplant slices with coarse salt and leave for 30 minutes. Rinse well and dry. Heat olive oil in a large pan and fry the eggplant slices in batches until golden brown. Do not let them become crisp. Drain on paper towels (kitchen paper) and allow to cool.

Roll the fresh pasta out into thin sheets. Cut out circles of 2¾ inches (7 cm). Put a slice of eggplant on each pasta circle and dot ½ teaspoon tomato sauce on top. Cover this with a round of mozzarella, ½ teaspoon tomato sauce, and another slice of eggplant. Cover with another circle of pasta and seal well round the edges. Continue in this way until you have 2 tortelli per person.

Cook the tortelli in a large pot of salted boiling water until they float to the top of the water. Lift out gently and dress with butter, Parmesan, and remaining tomato sauce. Decorate with basil leaves and serve.

Ravioli con Ripieno di Carciofi
Ravioli with Artichoke Filling

Although many fresh pasta shops make pasta stuffed with artichokes, their filling tends to be white, with more ricotta cheese than artichoke. I like to make these large ravioli with a wonderful dark green filling. This recipe makes about twelve to fifteen ravioli.

FRESH PASTA

2 cups (298 g) all-purpose (plain) flour

Pinch of salt

1 teaspoon (5 mL) extra virgin olive oil

3 eggs, beaten

2 egg yolks, beaten

FILLING

6 artichokes, trimmed and cut into quarters (see page 119)

1 small onion, chopped

Salt to taste

12 leaves mint

2 tablespoons (14 g) freshly grated Parmesan cheese

To make the pasta, mix together the flour and salt in a mixing bowl. Add the oil and then the eggs and egg yolks. Mix well and knead on a lightly floured surface until you have a smooth, elastic dough. I use my electric mixer with dough hook, but I like to finish kneading by hand because it is such a satisfying feeling. Put the dough in a lightly oiled bowl and cover. Leave to rest for 30 minutes.

Meanwhile, make the filling. Put the artichokes, onion, and salt in a medium saucepan and cover with boiling water. Cook until soft, about 15 minutes. Drain well and, using a blender or food processor, purée with the mint leaves and Parmesan. Allow to cool.

Roll out the pasta into very thin rectangular strips. I use a small pasta machine for

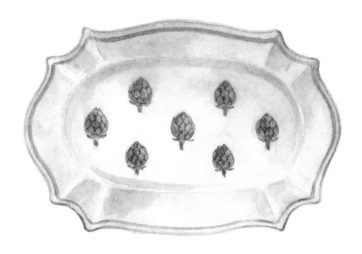

4 tablespoons (57 g)
butter, melted

2 tablespoons (14 g)
freshly grated
Parmesan

4 sprigs mint

Black pepper to taste

this, and do one sheet at a time. Cut each of the strips into 2 identical lengths. At regular intervals, place a large spoonful of the artichoke mixture on one half of the strip and cover with the other half. Using a pastry wheel cutter, cut into large ravioli measuring about 2½ inches (6 cm) square. Place the ravioli on a floured baking sheet (baking tray) so that they are not touching, and make the second batch in the same way. Keep in a cool place until ready to eat.

Cook the ravioli in a large pan of salted, boiling water until they float to the top of the water. Remove carefully with a slotted spoon and serve on individual plates with melted butter, Parmesan, a sprig of mint, and salt and pepper.

Gnocchi al Basilico

Basil Gnocchi

Although traditional Roman gnocchi made with semolina are rather heavy, these basil gnocchi are very light, thanks to the ricotta cheese. They are easily made and cook in a matter of minutes. We like to eat them in spring or early autumn with the last of the real basil grown in the open air. Hothouse basil does not have the same flavor.

10½ ounces (298 g) potatoes, boiled in their skins with a little salt

⅔ cup (142 g) fresh ricotta, drained for 1 hour

1 egg, beaten

½ cup (75 g) all-purpose (plain) flour

2 cups (57 g) basil leaves

1 clove garlic

½ cup (57 g) freshly grated Parmesan

Salt and black pepper to taste

4 tablespoons (57 g) butter, melted

8 leaves basil, roughly torn for garnish

Peel the potatoes while still hot and mash until quite smooth. Work in the ricotta, 1 tablespoon of the beaten egg, and the flour. Discard the remaining egg.

Blanch the basil leaves for a few seconds in boiling water, then dry thoroughly. In a blender or food processor, purée the garlic, basil leaves, and cheese. Knead into the potato mixture and add salt and pepper. Cover and refrigerate for 10 minutes.

Take small pieces of the potato mixture and, on a floured surface, roll into long cylinders as thick as your little finger. Cut into ½-inch (1-cm) lengths and roll slightly. I use a small indented board to form the gnocchi, but the back of a fork will do equally well. (In fact they taste just as good if they are smooth and not indented.) Put them on a floured baking sheet (baking tray) not touching each other.

When ready to eat, drop the gnocchi into salted boiling water. They are ready as soon as they float to the top. Lift out with a slotted spoon and serve with the butter and basil leaves.

Risotto di Asparagi

Asparagus Risotto

W*hen spring comes to Rome's vegetable markets the whole world seems charged with energy and good humor. In Campo dei Fiori the pace quickens, yet the rough edge is smoothed off many tongues, and when the inebriated would-be Pavarotti pauses in full throat of his third loud rendering of "O sole mio," to ask for a free avocado, he is brushed off with amused scorn. If he had asked for an Italian spring vegetable, he would probably have gotten it. Even those stalls selling imported, out-of-season vegetables subtly denigrate the fashionable world's sense of value, and when Maria proudly points out the first home-grown asparagus—"roba nostra!"—I know we both have her seal of approval.*

2 pounds (907 g) green
  asparagus

½ cup (118 mL) dry white
  wine

4 tablespoons (57 g) butter

1 shallot, finely chopped

1½ cups (298 g) Vialone,
  Carnaroli, or Arborio
  rice

4 tablespoons (30 g)
  freshly grated
  Parmesan cheese

Salt and black pepper
  to taste

Break the tough ends off the asparagus spears and discard. Cut off the extreme tips and coarsely chop the rest of the spears. Blanch the tips in lightly salted boiling water. Remove the tips with a slotted spoon and set aside. Cook the spears in the same water until soft. In a blender or food processor, purée the spears with their cooking water to make a thick stock, add wine, and keep simmering over low heat.

In a heavy pan, melt half the butter and gently cook the shallot until soft. Stir in the rice and let it begin to absorb the butter before adding a ladle of the asparagus stock. Stir until it is absorbed. Stir in the tips and add another ladle of stock. Keep adding the stock, a ladleful at a time, taking care not to "drown" the rice, until the rice is al dente, about 20 minutes. You may have to use some boiling water if the stock runs out. Stir in the remaining butter and the cheese, beat with a wooden spoon, cover, and leave to stand for 5 minutes. Check salt and serve with black pepper.

Risotto ai Carciofi

Artichoke Risotto

I have such a passion for artichokes I sometimes fear I might emulate Catherine de' Medici, who nearly died of a surfeit of artichokes after making a pig of herself at a wedding feast. Italian cooking uses artichokes in many guises, but is probably seen at its best in this princely risotto, which confirms the late Jane Grigson's opinion: "The artichoke above all is the vegetable expression of civilized living."

6 artichokes, cleaned and trimmed (see page 119)

4 tablespoons (59 mL) extra virgin olive oil

2 cups (473 mL) water

1 cup (237 mL) dry white wine

2 sprigs mint

Salt

1 small onion, finely chopped

1½ cups (298 g) Vialone, Carnaroli, or Arborio rice

1 cup (237 mL) light stock (see page 118), simmering

4 tablespoons (28 g) freshly grated Parmesan cheese

2 tablespoons (28 g) butter

6 leaves mint, finely chopped

Black pepper to taste

Cut 2 artichokes into thick segments and the remaining 4 into slices. Heat 1 tablespoon (15 mL) of the olive oil and fry the artichoke segments until golden brown. Using a slotted spoon, transfer to paper towels (kitchen paper) to drain. In a small saucepan, bring the water to a boil and add the wine, mint sprigs, artichoke slices, and salt to taste. Cook until tender. Drain the artichokes, reserving the cooking water for stock. Discard the mint.

In a heavy pan, heat the remaining oil and gently cook the onion until soft. Then stir in the rice and let it begin to absorb some of the oil. Now add a little of the reserved artichoke cooking water and some slices of artichoke, stirring all the time. As the stock is absorbed, stir in more cooking water and more artichokes. Continue in this way until the rice is al dente, about 20 minutes, switching to light stock when you have finished the cooking water. At this point stir in the cheese, butter, and mint leaves, and beat with a wooden spoon. Season with salt to taste, cover, and leave for 5 minutes.

Serve garnished with the fried artichoke segments, and with black pepper.

Supplì

Fried Rice Balls

These golden, egg-shaped rice balls are a favorite Roman snack. They are sold with pizza rustica, the pizza baked in great rectangular trays and sold by the slice, to be eaten at all hours of the day by anyone and everyone. The supplì are stuffed with mozzarella, and as you bite into the heart of the rice, strings of melted mozzarella keep you joined, just as the telephone "supply" links caller to called. I often make smaller versions to serve as nibbles with drinks.

RICE BALLS

2 cups (473 mL) light
   stock (see page 118)

4 tablespoons (57 g) butter

1 cup plus 2 tablespoons
   (255 g) Arborio rice

¾ cup (85 g) freshly
   grated Parmesan cheese

Pinch of freshly grated
   nutmeg

1 tablespoon chopped
   fresh parsley

2 eggs, beaten

3½ ounces (99 g)
   mozzarella, chopped

2 ounces (57 g) prosciutto,
   chopped (optional)

COATING

Flour for dusting

2 eggs, beaten

Dried bread crumbs

———

Olive oil for frying

Put the stock on to boil. Meanwhile, melt the butter in a large pan. Stir in the rice and gradually add the boiling stock, stirring constantly until the liquid is absorbed as for risotto. When the rice is al dente, remove from heat. Stir in half the Parmesan, the nutmeg, and parsley. Spread the rice mixture out on a large plate or work surface and allow to cool. When it is cold, stir in the eggs and the rest of the Parmesan.

Form small balls of the rice mixture and, with your thumb, make a cavity in the middle of each. Stuff this with a piece of mozzarella and a piece of ham and close the hole by smoothing round the rice. Shape the balls into smooth egg shapes and dust each with flour. Dip each in beaten egg and bread crumbs, and keep in the cool for 30 minutes to set the coating.

When ready to eat, heat oil in a heavy saucepan and fry the rice balls in batches until golden brown. Remove with a slotted spoon and serve at once.

Minestra di Broccoli alla Romana
Broccoli Broth with Pancetta, Prosciutto, and Pasta

I vividly remember the first time I tried this comforting minestra, *since it was also the first time I understood* l'arte di arrangiarsi, *the Roman code for adapting to fit the prevailing situation. My car had been towed away and after I had located the car pound, pushed at the post office to pay the fine, and limped back to the pound to wave my receipt, I was greeted with* "Documenti" *(papers). I dug out my British driving license, passport, and the Italian logbook for the car. Disaster. The logbook was in my unmarried name, as required by Italian law; the others, in my married name. With incipient schizophrenia I pleaded that we were both called "Diane," both born in London on the same day. I tried reason, explanations, indignation. To no avail. Finally, I burst into tears. Immediately, everything was resolved. The car release was signed and the official insisted on escorting me to a trattoria and ordering a plate of* minestra *to soothe my nerves, before he would dream of letting me drive home. As I sat hiccuping my way through the steaming dish I realized I had learned a magic button to be pushed in emergencies. Tears.*

14 ounces (397 g) broccoli, washed and trimmed

Salt to taste

2 tablespoons (30 mL) olive oil

3 ½ ounces (99 g) pancetta or bacon, chopped

1 small onion, chopped

1 small dried chile pepper

2 cloves garlic, crushed

3 ½ ounces (99 g) prosciutto, chopped

7 ounces (198 g) spaghetti, broken into short lengths

¼ cup (28 g) freshly grated pecorino cheese

Divide the broccoli into florets, cutting off and discarding the tough pieces of stalk. Cook in 4 cups (about 1 L) lightly salted boiling water until just tender. Drain the broccoli, reserving the cooking liquid.

In a large pan, heat the oil and add the pancetta, onion, chile, and garlic. When they begin to turn golden brown, stir in the prosciutto and broccoli water. Bring to a boil and cook the pasta until al dente. Return the broccoli to the pan, adjust seasoning, and serve with a liberal sprinkling of pecorino cheese.

Minestra di Pasta e Ceci

Pasta and Chickpeas

*I*n the past this dish was served on days that the Church decreed magro, or when meat was not to be eaten, and even today this dish is often eaten on Fridays, or the vigilia, *the day before an important religious holiday. The chickpeas must be soaked overnight.*

7 ounces (198 g) dried
   chickpeas

¼ cup (59 mL) olive oil

1 clove garlic, minced

1 teaspoon rosemary
   leaves, chopped

2 tablespoons (30 mL)
   fresh tomato sauce
   (see page 118) diluted
   with ½ cup (118 mL)
   boiling water

Salt and black pepper
   to taste

7 ounces (198 g) dried
   pasta, preferably fettuccine, broken into short
   lengths

Soak the chickpeas overnight. Drain, place in a large saucepan, add 6 cups (1.4 L) cold water, cover, and bring to a boil. Lower heat and cook gently until very soft, about 1 hour. (The traditional recipes specify 4 hours, but today's chickpeas rarely need more than 1 hour.)

In a large pan, heat the oil and gently cook the garlic and rosemary until the garlic begins to change color. Add the tomato sauce diluted with the boiling water.

Purée half the chickpea mixture in a blender or food processor, then stir into the remaining chickpeas and cooking liquid. Stir in the garlic and tomato mixture, check seasoning, and add salt and pepper to taste. Bring to a boil and throw in the pasta. Cook until the pasta is al dente, then serve at once. (If you are using pasta made without egg, it will take longer to cook, so stir the *minestra* from time to time to prevent it from sticking to the bottom of the pan.) It is not usual to serve grated cheese with this dish.

Stracciatella

This had always seemed an insipid, uninspiring soup until I tasted the home-made version at a christening in Marcellina, a small village just outside Rome. The mother celebrated the arrival of her long-awaited baby, Angelo, by preparing every course herself, and for this soup the eggs were still warm from her hens, and the stock had the same impeccable pedigree. It was ambrosia. To avoid disappointment, cook this soup only with superb, fresh ingredients.

4 eggs

¼ cup (28 g) freshly
   grated Parmesan cheese

¼ cup (28 g) coarse-
   ground semolina

Pinch of salt

Pinch of nutmeg

4 cups (946 mL) cold light
   stock (see page 118)

Beat the eggs together with the cheese, semolina, salt, and nutmeg. Add a ladle of cold stock. Bring the remaining stock to a boil, remove from the heat, and whisk in the egg mixture until the soup is full of uniform threads. Simmer gently for a few minutes, whisking continuously, then check the seasoning and serve very hot.

Passato di Peperoni Gialli
Yellow Pepper Soup

I learned this recipe many years ago from Benedetta Vitali of Cibreo restaurant in Florence. It became a firm favorite here in Rome, and I love to cook it in the early autumn when the Roman peppers (capsicums) are so good. The soup is a lovely bright yellow, and looks as good as it tastes.

2 tablespoons (30 mL)
   extra virgin olive oil

1 onion, finely chopped

1 carrot, finely chopped

1 stalk celery, finely
   chopped

4 yellow bell peppers
   (capsicums), seeded,
   ribs removed, and
   coarsely chopped

4 potatoes, peeled and
   coarsely chopped

4 cups (946 mL) light
   stock (see page 118)

Salt and black pepper to
   taste

1 cup (237 mL) milk

2 bay leaves

1 tablespoon freshly
   grated Parmesan

In a large pan, heat the oil and gently fry the onion, carrot, and celery until golden brown. Add the peppers and potatoes and stir-fry for a few minutes before adding enough stock to just cover the vegetables. Add salt and pepper. Cover and simmer for about 25 minutes.

Pass the mixture through a food mill to remove the pepper skins, then purée in a blender or food processor until smooth. Return to heat, adding the milk, bay leaves, and a little more stock if necessary. The soup should be liquid but creamy. Do not allow the soup to boil. Remove the bay leaves and serve hot with a little Parmesan spooned over a small part of the surface.

Zuppa di Funghi
Mushroom Soup

This soup can be made with any combination of fresh mushrooms available, but I try to use at least one or two wild mushrooms for the extra flavor they give.

3 cups (710 mL) light
   stock (see page 118)

3 tablespoons (44 mL)
   extra virgin olive oil

1 onion, finely sliced

1 ounce (28 g) pancetta or
   bacon, diced

10½ ounces (298 g) mixed
   mushrooms, sliced

10½ ounces (298 g) pota-
   toes, peeled and cubed

1 tablespoon chopped
   fresh parsley

Salt and black pepper
   to taste

4 slices stale coarse bread
   (optional)

In a saucepan, bring the stock to a boil. Meanwhile, heat half the oil in a large pan and gently cook the onion and pancetta until soft. Add the mushrooms, stirring around the pan for 5 minutes. Now add the boiling stock, potatoes, parsley, salt, and pepper. Simmer for 20 minutes. Using the back of a wooden spoon, mash some of the potato cubes. Taste and adjust the seasoning with salt and pepper.

This soup is often served ladled over a slice of bread fried in olive oil, but this can be omitted if preferred. If you want to use the bread, fry it quickly in the remaining 1½ tablespoons olive oil just before serving.

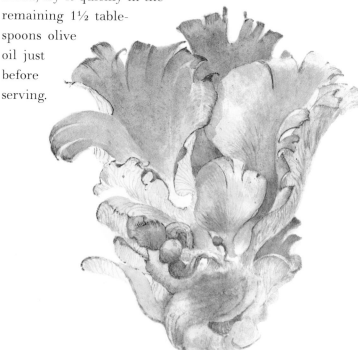

Zuppa di Castagne e Porcini

Chestnut and Porcini Mushroom Soup

In autumn in Rome the markets sell dried, shelled chestnuts that make life much easier when it comes to soups and stuffings. However, the masochist in me is convinced that the soup tastes better when made with burned fingers.

1 pound (454 g) chestnuts

6 cups (1.4 L) light stock (see page 118), cooked with 3 additional celery stalks

2 tablespoons (30 mL) olive oil

4 tablespoons (57 g) butter

1 cup (155 g) finely chopped onions

7 ounces (198 g) porcini mushrooms (cèpes, scraped, sponged, and sliced)

½ cup (118 mL) full-bodied red wine

Salt and black pepper to taste

Slit the chestnut shells at the base and soak for 10 minutes in boiling water. Remove from the water and peel off the shells. Boil the chestnuts in the stock until they are soft. In a blender or food processor, purée half the chestnuts with some of the stock, and crumble the remaining chestnuts to give some texture to the soup.

In a large pan, heat the oil and butter and gently stew the onions until they begin to change color. Add the mushrooms and cook gently until all their liquid is evaporated. Pour in the wine and cook until it is absorbed. Stir in the chestnut pieces, the chestnut purée, and the remaining stock. Cook for 10 minutes, check seasoning, add salt and pepper to taste, and serve hot.

Zuppa di Farro

Spelt Soup

Farro, or spelt, is a primitive wheat that was used in ancient Rome to make bread. It was the staple of the Roman army, and when it was replaced by modern wheat in bread making, it continued to be used in country areas for rustic soups. In the last few years it has enjoyed a revival, and last Christmas a fashionable hostess, serving zuppa di farro *at her party, assured me that it was now seen on all the best tables. It is a tasty, substantial soup ideal for cold winter evenings, belonging to the same tradition as the great Tuscan bean soups.*

2 tablespoons (30 mL)
  extra virgin olive oil,
  plus a little for garnish
  (optional)

2 slices pancetta or bacon,
  finely chopped
  (optional)

1 clove garlic, minced

1 onion, finely chopped

1 small dried chile
  pepper, crushed

3 small tomatoes, peeled,
  seeded, and chopped
  (see page 119)

1 stalk celery, finely
  chopped

1 carrot, finely chopped

4 cups (946 mL) light
  stock (see page 118)

1¼ (198 g) spelt, washed

Salt to taste

In a large pan, heat the oil. If using the pancetta, add it to the oil and slowly cook it, letting the fat melt out. Add the garlic, onion, and chile pepper, and cook until the garlic begins to change color. Add the tomatoes, celery, and carrot, and after 5 minutes pour in stock. Bring to a boil and stir in the spelt. Adjust seasoning with salt to taste, cover, lower heat, and cook gently for 30 minutes. The soup can be served with a swirl of fine olive oil on top if desired.

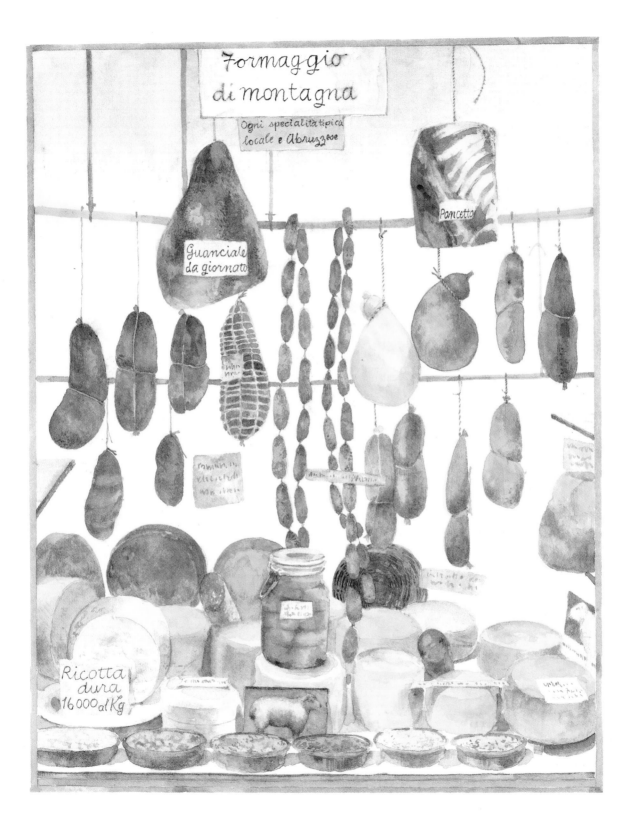

VEGETABLES

Romans have always loved fresh vegetables and herbs, and the city's favorable microclimate and plentiful water supply ensured top quality. As building grew and the countryside receded, Renaissance courtyards were turned into vegetable gardens, and at one time the best celery and artichokes were grown around the Trevi Fountain and Pincio. Streams were deflected to provide irrigation, and by the late sixteenth century a law had to be passed forbidding this practice since the city was literally awash.

Today few households have vegetable gardens, but most balconies are crowded with pots of herbs, and the street vegetable markets supply the constant demand for fresh greenery. Romans prize wild vegetables and herbs for their good flavor, and in season the stalls sell wild asparagus, chicory leaves, fennel, arugula (rocket), and salad leaves. Today the wild varieties cost more than the cultivated equivalent, since the picking is more labor-intensive.

In my local market I can buy washed spinach, trimmed broccoli, and green beans topped, tailed, and broken into uniform lengths. I enjoy shelling peas myself, but customers without time or inclination can buy little plastic bags of peas, fava and Borlotti beans, freshly shelled by the parents of the present stall holders. Artichokes, skillfully trimmed, bob about in a large pail of water and lemon juice, or for the more discerning customer they are cleaned to order. When the final purchase has been made, the vendor lovingly assembles a little bunch of selected herbs, the *odori*, which are given free to complete the transaction.

In the last few years, winters in Rome have been enhanced by the advent of the small red cherry tomato from Pachino in Sicily. In the past, Romans used bottled tomatoes in winter since the bland, flavorless hothouse variety appalled the sensibilities of the demanding Roman *gustaio*. Pachino tomatoes are picked and sold on the vine, and they are full of flavor. They have revolutionized Rome's winter cooking, and this is one of the many gastronomic luxuries regarded as a daily essential.

To make life easier, I give simple directions for preparing eggplant, peppers (capsicums), and artichokes on page 119.

Carciofi alla Giudia

Artichokes Jewish Style

*T*his *is another delectable dish Rome has inherited from the old ghetto. Although specialty restaurants seem to serve them nearly all the year, they are best made with very young artichokes. The central artichoke of the plant, the* cimarolo, *if available, is the best for this recipe.*

6 round young artichokes

1 or 2 lemons

4 tablespoons (59 mL) vinegar

Olive oil for deep-frying

Salt and black pepper to taste

Take off the coarse external leaves of the artichokes and trim and peel the stalks, leaving them ½ inch (1 cm) long. Rub the artichokes with the cut lemon and put in a bowl of vinegar and water to prevent them from discoloring. Heat the oil for deep-frying to 300°F (150°C). While it is heating, drain the artichokes, one at a time, and place each head down on a hard surface, pressing firmly so that the leaves open out like a flower.

Season the insides of the artichokes with salt and pepper and fry in batches in the hot oil. Keep them submerged with the back of a slotted spoon, and do not let the oil get too hot or the artichokes will not cook evenly. After 10 minutes, turn up the heat and let them turn golden brown in 350°F (180°C) oil. Standing well back, flick a little cold water on the artichokes to crisp the leaves. Using a slotted spoon, transfer to paper towels (kitchen paper) to drain. Keep warm. They can be served hot or at room temperature.

Carciofi alla Romana

Artichokes Roman Style

In the autumn in Rome we find the artichoke tinged with purple, the violette, *but in spring the large round romanesco artichokes from around Cerveteri come into season, and these are used for* carciofi alla romana. *Traditionally they are stuffed with the wild* mentuccia *or pennyroyal, but I prefer to use the true mint, known here as* menta romana.

6 artichokes

1 lemon, cut in half

3 tablespoons (44 mL) vinegar

1 tablespoon chopped fresh parsley

3 tablespoons chopped fresh mint

2 cloves garlic, minced

Salt to taste

6 tablespoons (89 mL) olive oil

½ cup (118 mL) dry white wine (optional)

6 tablespoons (89 mL) boiling water

Remove the tough outer leaves of the artichokes, leaving at least 2½ inches (6 cm) of stalk.

Using a very sharp knife, pare off the coarse upper part of the leaves while turning the artichoke round in your hand. Rub the artichokes with a lemon half at regular intervals to prevent discoloration. At the end of this the artichoke should be almost tulip shaped. Now cut off the tips so that the artichoke can be stood on its head. Put in a bowl of vinegar and water while preparing the other artichokes.

Mix together the herbs and garlic with a little salt and 1 tablespoon (15 mL) of the olive oil. Force open the leaves of one artichoke and remove the coarse "choke," known as the *pelo* in Rome, with a teaspoon. Spoon a little of the herb mixture into the cavity. Prepare all the artichokes in this way, then stand them in a deep, close-fitting narrow pan. Add the remaining oil, the wine, lemon half, a little salt, and the boiling water. Cover and stew gently for about 1 hour. This dish is usually prepared in advance and served at room temperature.

Insalata di Fagioli e Tonno
Borlotti Bean and Tuna Salad

A*lthough I usually make this as a summer starter, I have friends who prefer to add cold pasta, like penne, to make a one-dish meal. It can be prepared with dried or fresh beans, and white beans can be substituted if preferred.*

2 cups (255 g) shelled
   fresh borlotti beans or 1
   cup (198 g) dried beans

Salt to taste

2 tablespoons (30 mL)
   extra virgin olive oil

1 tablespoon (15 mL)
   fresh lemon juice

Black pepper to taste

7 ounces (198 g) tuna in
   olive oil (ventresca cut)

7 ounces (198 g) short
   pasta (optional)

1 tablespoon chopped
   fresh chives

Dried beans need to be soaked for several hours, preferably overnight. Cook the beans in boiling water until soft. When they are cooked add salt to taste. In a blender or food processor, purée half the beans with enough cooking liquid to make a thick, smooth cream. Blend in half the olive oil and lemon juice, and add black pepper to taste. Dress the whole beans with the remaining oil and lemon juice. Gently stir the tuna and whole beans together and arrange on a bed of creamed beans.

If using pasta, cook in a large pot of salted boiling water until al dente. Drain and cool under the cold tap. Dress with the creamed beans, and gently stir in the tuna and whole beans. Sprinkle over the chives and serve.

Fave e Pecorino

Fava Beans and Pecorino Cheese

This is the favorite Roman "starter" in spring when the first tender young fava beans appear. On May first, the public holiday for the workers, lorries drive up from the countryside south of Rome and tip out shining heaps of fresh beans to be sold by the side of the main roads leading out of Rome. This is traditionally a day for picnics or eating out, and even on elegant tables the fava beans are served in their pods. Everyone shells their own, and if you find a pod with nine beans you must keep it safe for it will bring you good luck for the following year. The fertile countryside in the south around Anagni is known as the Ciociara. In the past the farmers wore comfortable footwear called ciocie, which gave the area its name. The ciocie were square pieces of animal skin, wrapped round the foot and leg, and secured by cords and string wound around and around. Even today on May first some of the country vendors wear this comfortable homemade footwear.

2 pounds (907 g) tender young fava beans in the pod

7 ounces (198 g) pecorino cheese that is not too mature and salty

Place all the beans on the tablecloth in the middle of the table. Let your guests shell their own beans. Cut the pecorino into wedges and hand around.

Fave al Guanciale

Fava Beans and Bacon

Traditional Roman cooking was very heavy, and most of the recipes begin with a battuto *of fat bacon, or ham fat. For many recipes the initial cooking is done in the fat slowly melted from the* guanciale, *or the cheek of the pig. Today this is often replaced by pancetta or bacon, but upholders of authentic Roman cooking get quite aggressive about the "lowering of standards." In Campo dei Fiori, Viola, a* salumeria *established in 1890, sells all the traditional robust ingredients. They put their wrapped wares in plastic carrier bags colored a delicate mauve (*viola *in Italian) with a masterly display of sense and sensibility. It is not every day pigs' trotters get to look like lingerie!*

2 tablespoons (5 g) finely chopped guanciale, pancetta, or bacon

1 tablespoon finely chopped onion

1 pound (454 g) young fava beans, shelled

Salt and black pepper to taste

In a pan, gently melt the fat from the guanciale, then add the onion. Stir for a few moments, and as the onion begins to change color, add the beans. Stir around in the fat, and add just enough water to prevent them sticking to the bottom of the pan. Cover and simmer until tender. Add a little more water during cooking if necessary. Season to taste and serve.

Insalata di Fagiolini e Tonno

Green Bean and Tuna Salad

There is always a moment in summer when the only green vegetable available seems to be fagiolini. *They are often cooked with tomatoes to ring the changes, but I feel that the tomatoes take over. The tuna fish works well, and this can be prepared as a light lunch when it is too hot to cook, or an interesting antipasto.*

18 ounces (510 g) small,
   tender green beans,
   trimmed

2 tablespoons (30 mL)
   extra virgin olive oil

1 tablespoon (15 mL)
   fresh lemon juice

7 ounces (198 g) tuna in
   olive oil (ventresca cut),
   drained and flaked

2 thin scallions (spring
   onions), finely chopped

Salt and black pepper
   to taste

Cook the beans in salted boiling water until just beginning to be tender. Plunge into iced water to stop the cooking process and keep them a good color. Just before serving, drain, dress with oil and lemon juice, top with flaked tuna, and sprinkle the scallions over the top. Season to taste with salt and pepper.

Frittelle di Borraggine

Borage Fritters

This is another recipe I learned from Maria, in Campo dei Fiori market. Borage with its hairy leaves and bright blue flowers is a much-prized herb. In Liguria it is used to stuff pasta and it gives a great flavor to soups. It grows wild, but those of us who live in towns depend on the patient lore of the contadine, or farmers, who satisfy Rome's craving for fresh vegetables with all the flavor of a more leisurely age.

BATTER

1½ cups (198 g) all-
   purpose (plain) flour

2 teaspoons (10 g) baking
   powder

2 eggs, beaten

2 tablespoons (14 g)
   freshly grated
   Parmesan cheese

1 cup (237 mL) water

Salt and black pepper
   to taste

_____

12 large leaves borage
   or other leafy vegetable,
   shredded

Olive oil for deep-frying

Beat together the batter ingredients to make a thick batter. Leave to rest at room temperature for 2 hours.

Stir in the borage. In a large pan, heat the oil. Drop in spoonfuls of the mixture to make small fritters. Fry until golden brown. Cook in batches, and serve piping hot.

Cardi alla Parmigiana

Baked Cardoons with Parmesan

Cardoons, a type of edible thistle, are a favorite Roman winter vegetable. In ancient Rome, when the artichoke was not known, cardoons were consumed in great quantities. In Rome today they have a shorter season than artichokes and they are less versatile. This recipe can be made with artichokes if cardoons are not available. I dedicate this recipe to Clarissa, who loves cardoons in any guise!

1½ pounds (681 g) cardoons, trimmed, scraped and cut into 4-inch (10-cm) lengths

Salt and black pepper to taste

Juice of 2 lemons

Flour for dredging

2 eggs, beaten

Olive oil for frying

2 cups (473 mL) fresh tomato sauce (see page 118)

¾ cup (74 g) freshly grated Parmesan cheese

2 tablespoons (28 g) butter

With cardoons it is essential to trim well and scrape off all the tough strings. Leave them in a mixture of cold water, salt and pepper, and lemon juice for 15 minutes to keep them white. Some people prefer to sprinkle them with flour to keep them from floating to the top. Rinse, then cook in salted boiling water until nearly tender, about 30 minutes. Drain well, pat dry with paper towels (kitchen paper), dip first in flour and then in beaten eggs.

Preheat the oven to 350°F (175°C/gas mark 4). In a large pan heat olive oil. Fry the cardoon pieces until golden brown. Using a slotted spoon, transfer to paper towels (kitchen paper) to drain, then combine with the hot tomato sauce and grated cheese. Put in an oven dish, dot with butter, and bake for 15 minutes.

Broccoli "Strascinati" in Padella
Broccoli Roman Style

Traditionally in Rome this dish uses the pungent green broccolo romano, which is literally "dragged into the frying pan." The same effect can be achieved by using cauliflower, broccoli, or a mixture of the two.

1 large untrimmed broccoli or cauliflower, or
1 small cauliflower and
1 small untrimmed broccoli, 2 pounds
(907 g) in all

¼ cup (59 mL) extra virgin olive oil

2 cloves garlic, finely chopped

1 small dried chile pepper, crushed

Salt to taste

Trim the broccoli and/or cauliflower, discarding the tough stalks and outer leaves of the broccoli. Divide into small florets or sprigs.

In a large pan with a lid, heat the oil and stir in the broccoli and/or cauliflower, garlic, chile pepper, and a little salt. Cover and cook very gently, stirring frequently. It may be necessary to add a sprinkling of water towards the end, but the best results come from a judicious combination of frying and steaming. Do not drown the vegetables.

Serve on a separate plate to accompany any grilled or roast meat, or serve as a healthy alternative on its own.

Cicoria all'Agro

Wild Chicory with Olive Oil and Lemon Juice

Romans *love these bitter wild leaves, and the markets sell them already washed and trimmed. This simple way of dressing cooked vegetables can be used for many greens, including spinach, cauliflower, and asparagus.*

**2 pounds (907 g)
   wild chicory, cut and
   trimmed**

Fresh lemon juice to taste

**Extra virgin olive oil
   to taste**

Cook the chicory by plunging it into salted boiling water. When it begins to become tender, drain and plunge into iced water so that the cooking stops and it retains a good color. Drain well. When ready to serve, dress with lemon and oil.

Puntarelle in Salsa di Alici

Catalonian Chicory in Anchovy Sauce

For this dish you need the wild asparagus-family chicory. It is one of Rome's favorite salads, and in the markets the older stall holders sit preparing great curly mounds. The dressing can also be used for other bitter greens.

18 ounces (510 g)
   puntarelle, washed and
   trimmed

1 clove garlic, chopped

4 anchovy fillets, chopped

2 tablespoons (30 mL)
   white wine vinegar

¼ cup (59 mL) extra
   virgin olive oil

Salt and black pepper
   to taste

Cut the puntarelle stalks lengthwise into thin strips and put them in a bowl of cold water until they curl up. Although traditionally the anchovy sauce was made by pounding in a mortar, you can use a blender or a food processor. Purée the garlic, anchovies, and vinegar. With the machine running, slowly pour in the oil. Check for seasoning; you will need pepper but the anchovies will probably provide enough salt. Toss the puntarelle and dress with the sauce. Serve at once.

Tortini di Polenta

Corn Blini

This mixture can be used in many ways. I like to make small bases 2½ inches (6 cm) in diameter and serve them as nibbles. They can be topped with the mushroom mixture used in Panzerotti ai Finferli (page 58), smoked salmon and/or caviar, or thin slices of eggplant (aubergine) and mozzarella, as given below.

2 thin eggplants (aubergines), cut into fine slices

Coarse salt for sprinkling

Olive oil for frying

BLINI

⅓ cup (57 g) polenta

⅓ cup (57 g) corn flour

Pinch of salt

¼ ounce (7 g) fresh yeast or 1 teaspoon active dried yeast

½ cup (118 mL) tepid milk

⅔ cup (159 mL) sour cream or thick yogurt

1 egg, separated, the yolk beaten and the white reserved

Butter for cooking

7 ounces (198 g) mozzarella, cut into thin 1½-inch (4-cm) rounds

6 small cherry tomatoes, cut in half

Sprigs of basil for garnish

Sprinkle the eggplant slices with coarse salt and let sit for 30 minutes. Rinse and dry well. Heat oil in a large pan and fry the eggplant slices until pale golden brown. Using a slotted spatula, transfer to paper towels (kitchen paper) to drain and keep warm.

To make the blini, mix together the polenta, corn flour, and pinch of salt. Mix the yeast with a little tepid milk. Heat the remaining milk and the sour cream or yogurt until warm, add the egg yolk, and stir into the yeast. Pour this into the polenta mixture and mix to make a smooth batter. Cover with a cloth and leave for 1 hour in a warm, draft-free place.

Whip the egg white until stiff peaks form and fold into the batter. Cover and leave for 1 hour or longer.

Preheat the oven to 400°F (200°C/gas mark 6).

In a large pan, melt a little butter and cook 3 or 4 blini at a time on both sides without browning. Keep warm.

On each blini, arrange a slice of eggplant, a round of mozzarella, and a tomato half. Heat in the oven for 5 minutes. Decorate with basil and serve.

Marignani Marinati

Marinated Eggplant

Although the Italian for eggplant (aubergine) is melanzane, *in Rome they used to be called* marignani, *and some lovers of good food still insist on this name. In the last century the clergymen sent by the Vatican on special missions out of the city were known as* marignani, *after the swirling aubergine-colored cloaks wrapped round their shoulders. Romans traditionally love to poke fun at all authority!*

4 unpeeled eggplants (aubergines), diced

Salt for sprinkling

Olive oil for frying

1 cup (237 mL) white wine vinegar

3 cloves garlic, finely chopped

1 small dried chile pepper

Sprinkle the eggplant with salt and let sit for about 1 hour. Rinse well and dry.

In a large pan, heat olive oil and fry eggplant slices until golden brown. Remove with a slotted spoon and drain on paper towels (kitchen paper) to absorb any surplus oil. Transfer to a deep plate.

In a small saucepan, heat the vinegar, garlic, and chile pepper and allow to boil for a few minutes. Leave the mixture to cool before pouring over the eggplant. Marinate for 2 or 3 days, stirring from time to time. Serve with the marinade as an antipasto, or with grilled poultry or meat.

Gratinata di Porri e Zucchini
Baked Leeks and Zucchini

The Roman poet Horace speaks of a tasty dish with leeks, but over the centuries leeks were forgotten in Rome. About twenty years ago they appeared again at one stall in Testaccio market. I remember getting there early on Saturday mornings, before they were sold out, and explaining to curious local shoppers how I used them. Now they are again found all over the city, and imaginative modern cooks like to use the tender long leaves to wrap up elegant seafood morsels. In this recipe they are combined with the last zucchini (courgettes) of the season, and baked with a cheesy crust.

4 leeks, trimmed and finely sliced

4 zucchini (courgettes), diced

2 eggs, beaten

¾ cup plus 2 tablespoons (207 mL) milk

1 ounce (28 g) freshly grated Parmesan cheese

1 slice prosciutto, diced (optional)

Salt and black pepper to taste

1 tablespoon (7 g) dried bread crumbs

2 tablespoons (28 g) butter

Preheat the oven to 400°F (200°C/gas mark 6).

Steam the leeks and zucchini over boiling water for 3 minutes. Keep warm. Beat together the eggs, milk, and half the cheese, then add the prosciutto, vegetables, salt, and pepper. Transfer to an oven dish and sprinkle with remaining cheese and bread crumbs. Dot with butter and bake for 15 minutes.

PANTHEON

Panzerotti ai Finferli

Little Pies with Wild Mushrooms

Not many people still eat these traditional Roman small pastries stuffed with pork or offal. I like to cook them in October, using the lovely yellow chanterelle mushrooms. I serve them before dinner with a fragrant glass of Ribolla Gialla. These little panzerotti *are usually deep-fried and served hot, but they can be baked if you prefer.*

Pastry dough
 (see page 82)

2 tablespoons (30 mL)
 extra virgin olive oil,
 plus olive oil for deep-
 frying (optional)

10½ ounces (298 g) wild
 mushrooms, brushed,
 sponged, and chopped

1 clove garlic, finely
 chopped

1 tablespoon chopped
 fresh parsley

2 tablespoons (30 mL)
 heavy (double) cream
 or mascarpone cheese

Salt and black pepper
 to taste

If baking the pastries, preheat the oven to 350°F (175°C/gas mark 4).

Roll out the pastry and cut into 2½-inch (6-cm) diameter circles.

In a large pan, heat the oil and gently cook the mushrooms for a few minutes. Stir in the garlic, parsley, cream, salt, and pepper. Allow to thicken slightly before removing from heat. Leave to cool.

Spoon a little filling onto the pastry circles, then fold each over to make a half moon. Seal the edges well. If frying, fry the pastries until golden brown. Using a slotted spoon, transfer to paper towels (kitchen paper) to drain. If baking, arrange on a baking sheet and bake.

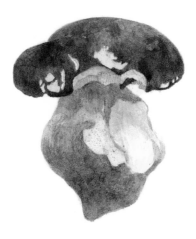

Cipolline in Agrodolce

Small Onions in Sweet-Sour Sauce

During the days of the Roman Empire hedonism reigned supreme, and Petronius's Satyricon describes opulent culinary extravaganzas. The combination of sweet and sour flavors still exists in many traditional dishes.

In Rome's markets it is possible to buy small bags of onions already peeled, which makes this dish very quick and easy.

18 ounces (510 g) cipolline or pearl (boiling) onions, peeled

2 tablespoons (28 g) prosciutto fat, or 2 tablespoons (30 mL) extra virgin olive oil

2 teaspoons sugar

⅓ cup (78 mL) red wine vinegar

1 teaspoon cornstarch (cornflour)

⅓ cup (78 mL) light stock (see page 118)

Salt and black pepper to taste

2 teaspoons (10 mL) traditionally made balsamic vinegar (optional)

Soak the cipolline in cold water for at least 30 minutes, then drain.

In a large pan, heat the fat or olive oil and stir in the sugar. After 3 minutes add the onions, stirring them round in the sugar. Pour in the vinegar and simmer until the onions are soft. Mix the cornstarch to a smooth paste with the stock and stir into the onions. Allow to thicken, season with salt and pepper to taste, and transfer to a serving dish. If you have any good balsamic vinegar, drizzle a little over the onions just before serving.

Frittata di Pasqua

Easter Frittata

In the past, eggs were a valuable source of income, and traditionally the egg and cheese money belonged to the women. They used the eggs themselves for special occasions, and this "extravagant" six-egg frittata was prepared for Easter.

2 tablespoons (30 mL) extra virgin olive oil

1 small onion, finely chopped

1 tablespoon freshly grated pecorino or Parmesan cheese

6 eggs, beaten

Salt and black pepper to taste

1 tablespoon chopped fresh parsley

2 tablespoons chopped fresh mint or mentuccia (European pennyroyal)

In a large pan, heat the oil and gently cook the onion until soft. Meanwhile, beat the cheese into the eggs and add salt and pepper. Stir the herbs into the onion, then pour the egg mixture over the onion and herbs, tilting the pan and lifting up the edges so that the liquid egg runs underneath. Cook until golden brown on both sides.

Peperoni alla Romana

Roman-Style Sweet Peppers

*T*his can be made with red or green bell peppers (capsicums), or a mixture of the two. The red peppers are sweet, while the green peppers have a rather bitter flavor. Romans tend to like bitter vegetables, like the wild cicoria (chicory) so popular here.

6 bell peppers
  (capsicums), roasted
  and peeled (see
  page 119)

¼ cup (59 mL) olive oil

1 onion, finely sliced

3 tomatoes, peeled and
  seeded (see page 119)

Salt and black pepper
  to taste

Cut the peppers into strips about 1 inch (2.5 cm) wide.

In a large pan over low heat, heat the oil and gently cook the onion until soft. Add the tomatoes, salt, and black pepper, and simmer for 10 minutes. Stir in the pepper strips, cook gently for a few minutes, then remove from the heat. These are usually served at room temperature.

Patate alla Contadina

Country-Style Potatoes

I use this quick potato recipe as a side dish, but in the south of Italy a similar combination is often used to dress pasta, and I have a vegetarian friend who eats it as a main dish.

3 tablespoons (44 mL)
  extra virgin olive oil

1 small onion, sliced

1 clove garlic, finely
  chopped

1 small dried chile
  pepper, crushed

18 ounces (510 g) pota-
  toes, peeled and thinly
  sliced

3 ripe tomatoes,
  peeled and sliced
  (see page 119)

1 tablespoon chopped
  fresh parsley

Salt to taste

In a large pan, heat the oil and gently fry the onion, garlic, and chile. Add the potatoes, tomatoes, and parsley and let them absorb the oil before adding salt and just enough water to cover them. Cover and simmer until the potatoes are tender. If you are using them to dress pasta, cook them a little longer until they are really soft.

Sformato di Patate

Souffléed Potatoes

I find it very difficult to work with a food photographer, because I can't bear to cook food that is not going to be eaten. I always want my food to be eaten at just the right moment, and I have learned to avoid domestic strife by calling out "wash your hands now!" as I open the oven. For this reason I like molded dishes that look good without needing time for decoration.

18 ounces (510 g)
  unpeeled potatoes

7 tablespoons (99 g)
  butter, melted

4 egg yolks, beaten

½ cup (57 g) freshly
  grated Parmesan cheese

Salt and black pepper
  to taste

4 egg whites, whipped to
  stiff peaks

Preheat the oven to 300°F (150°C/gas mark 2).

Boil the potatoes in salted water in their skins so they do not absorb too much water. Drain and mash with the butter. Beat in the egg yolks, Parmesan, salt, and pepper. Fold in the egg whites and spoon into small oiled molds. Place the molds in a baking pan and add hot water halfway up the sides of the molds. Bake for 20 minutes.

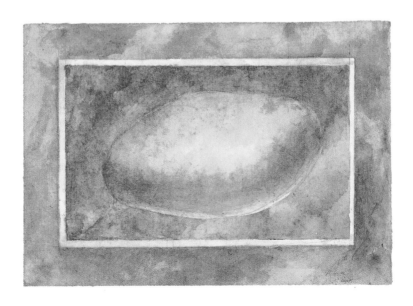

Pomodori con la Pasta

Tomatoes Stuffed with Pasta

My family loves this recipe, which is cooked in the summer when the large tomatoes are so full of flavor. The dried pasta shaped like cuffs is called avemaria, *as the cuffs are much in evidence when you lift up your hands to pray. In Rome the Church and good food have a great affinity, and if you see a table of priests at a trattoria, you are sure to eat well.*

4 large firm tomatoes

4 tablespoons (59 mL)
    extra virgin olive oil

1 clove garlic, minced

1 tablespoon chopped
    fresh parsley

Salt and black pepper
    to taste

½ cup (57 g) small dried
    shaped pasta, preferably
    avemaria or tubettini

2 tablespoons (28 g)
    freshly grated Parme-
    san cheese

8 leaves basil, torn to
    pieces

Preheat oven to 350°F (180°C/gas mark 4).

Carefully slice off the top of each tomato and keep to one side to act as lids. Scoop out the middles without piercing the skin, and sieve the pulp to remove the seeds. In a large pan, heat 3 tablespoons (44 mL) of the olive oil. Add the garlic, parsley, and tomato pulp, and gently cook until the garlic begins to change color. Season with salt and pepper.

Cook the pasta in a large pot of salted boiling water for half the stated cooking time. Drain and stir in the Parmesan and garlic sauce. Gently spoon the pasta into the tomatoes, tucking some basil in the middle. Add a few drops of the remaining 1 tablespoon of oil and put the "lids" on top. When all the tomatoes are stuffed, drizzle on the remaining oil and put in a close-fitting oven dish. Bake for 20 minutes.

Fiori di Zucca Fritti

Zucchini Flowers in Batter

These delicious flowers are usually served in Roman trattorias around the old ghetto, together with fillets of baccalà and artichokes Jewish style. I often make them to hand round for pre-dinner drinks. The same batter can be used for broccoli or cauliflower florets that have been previously parboiled in salted water. Other vegetables, like zucchini (courgettes), can be cut in batons, then dipped in batter and fried.

BATTER

½ ounce (14 g) fresh yeast or 2 teaspoons active dried yeast

1 tablespoon (15 mL) tepid water

1¼ cup (198 g) all-purpose (plain) flour

1 egg and 1 egg yolk, beaten together

1 teaspoon salt

2 tablespoons (30 mL) extra virgin olive oil

1 teaspoon (5 mL) dry white wine

———

8 zucchini (courgette) flowers, stalks, stamens, and pistils removed

2 anchovy fillets, chopped

8 sticks of mozzarella

Olive oil for frying

Salt to taste

To make the batter, dissolve the yeast in the tepid water. Beat together the flour, egg and egg yolk, salt, olive oil, and wine, then stir in the yeast mixture. Cover and leave in a warm place for 1 to 2 hours.

Gently part the flower petals and put in some anchovy and a stick of mozzarella. Fold the petals together and dip into the batter. In a large pan, heat the oil until hot. Holding the tip of each flower, lower them into the hot oil and fry until golden brown. I usually cook them in batches, and they must be eaten piping hot and lightly salted.

Misticanza

Wild Salad Leaves

*I*n the past, bunches of wild herbs for salad were left by the Cappuccini monks in return for alms. In Italy today, older country women can sit down in a field and, without getting to their feet, gather together a rich assortment of salad leaves in a few minutes. For those of us who have not acquired this skill the Roman markets sell a selection of leaves, or misticanza. They are usually dressed with salt, vinegar, and oil, but some people include chopped anchovy fillets or, in season, peeled grapes. The judicious combining of the dressing ingredients is all-important. There is an old proverb that says: "To dress a salad well you need four people. A wise man to put in the salt, a miser to add the vinegar, a spendthrift to pour in the oil, and a madman to toss it together."

Mixed wild green leaves, including if possible borage, arugula (rocket), dandelion, pimpernel, wild chicory, and so on to serve four (or more)

Extra virgin olive oil

White wine vinegar

Salt to taste

2 anchovy fillets, chopped (optional)

Peeled white grapes (optional)

Wash and dry greens. Combine all ingredients in a large salad bowl, toss, and serve.

FISH & SHELLFISH

Present-day Romans love to eat fish, and it is quite usual to have a meal in which the antipasto, pasta, and main course are all based on seafood. In this they are worthy descendants of the ancient Romans, who dedicated the fourth and fifth level of Trajan's Market to fish, with great fresh- and saltwater tanks to keep the fish alive until the last possible moment. At ancient fish farms the fish were overfed until they reached grotesque proportions, since the Romans of those days seem to have prized size above flavor. With the barbarian invasions this gastronomic culture disappeared, but the love of fish endured, and until 1922 the fish market near the Portico di Ottavia in Sant'Angelo in Pescheria sold a wide variety of seafood, with the River Tiber providing salmon, sturgeon, and caviar until the end of the nineteenth century. Given this consuming passion for fish I have always had my doubts about the motives behind the Church of Rome's interpretation of fasting. In the past it was forbidden to eat meat on Friday, but fish was allowed. Today, when this ban no longer applies, the Roman fishmongers continue to do a brisk trade on Fridays. In the same way, the feast days before Lent were called *carnevale,* or "farewell to meat," but since most Roman celebratory meals are based on fish in preference to meat, it is difficult to see the sacrifice being made.

Today the Tiber is hopelessly polluted, but the lakes and streams just outside Rome provide trout, whitefish, and other delicacies. Sturgeon is farmed in the Po to the north of Italy, and Italian caviar can be found in Rome. Salmon has become very popular, and since it is farmed it is less expensive than wild sea bass and bream.

Fiumicino, the site of Rome's airport, is the fishing port, and stalls along the quay sell a large variety of Mediterranean seafood. The fish auction takes place in the afternoon, and early evening sees the freshest catch. The fish shops in nearby Ostia have a system that allows you to reserve your place in the evening queue by buying a numbered ticket during the day. When the lorries arrive at about 6 PM, you get to choose what you want in numerical order. There is an air of excited expectancy as the unloading takes place, and I usually get carried away and buy too much, because in the center of Rome prices are much higher and there is less choice. The shrimp here have distinctive bright turquoise eggs, but I have never seen these in Rome fish markets. They are snapped up in the first few hours. In Rome the fish stalls and shops are only open in the morning, and some stalls sell their remaining fish to the larger supermarkets that are open in the afternoon.

Fish is cooked very simply with olive oil, seasoning, and herbs. It is usually cooked whole on the bone, and Roman waiters are expert at skimming over the fish with two spoons, lifting off the fillets at the speed of light. Until fairly recently the raw fish were displayed on a tray and carried from table to table, so that the customer could inspect the eyes and gills before making his choice. Today's modern recipes often use filleted fish, but they are served with a dressing of fresh vegetables, herbs, and olive oil. Heavy cream sauces play no part in Roman fish cooking. For this reason it is essential to use good, fresh ingredients.

Coregoni al Forno

Baked Lake Fish

O*utside Rome, in the crater of an extinct volcano, we find Lake Bracciano. The lake is rich in freshwater fish, and one of the great delicacies served by local trattorias is baked* coregone. *The local fishermen like to say mysteriously that the* coregone *is really a saltwater fish, and nobody knows how it came to be in this land-locked lake. I am grateful to Alan Davidson for his explanation that although the family is essentially freshwater, two of the species come out into Baltic, Arctic, and Canadian waters.*

2 lemons

4 fresh sage leaves, chopped

1 teaspoon chopped fresh rosemary leaves

1 clove garlic, finely chopped

4 coregoni (whitefish), weighing about 9 ounces (255 g) each, cleaned and scaled

1 tablespoon (15 mL) extra virgin olive oil

Salt and black pepper to taste

1 tablespoon chopped fresh parsley

Preheat the oven to 400°F (200°C/gas mark 6).

Slice one of the lemons into thin rounds and set aside. Cut the other lemon in half and remove the zest from one half. Mince the zest and mix it with the sage, rosemary, and garlic. Cut the remaining half lemon into wedges to serve with the cooked fish.

Brush a baking sheet large enough to contain all four fish in a single layer with olive oil and arrange the slices of lemon so that they will fit under each fish. Season the inside of each fish with salt and pepper and spoon in the parsley. Place the fish on top of the lemon slices and sprinkle on the rosemary mixture. Season with salt and pepper and drizzle on the remaining olive oil. Bake for 15 minutes.

Triglie con Pinoli e Uva Passa

Red Mullet with Raisins and Pine Nuts

This sweet and sour recipe is traditionally served by Roman Jewish families on Yom Kippur, the Day of Atonement. It is simple to prepare and quite delicious. It can be adapted to other small fish if red mullet are not readily available.

2 ounces (57 g) golden raisins (sultanas)

2 tablespoons (30 mL) extra virgin olive oil

4 or 8 whole red mullet (1 or 2 per serving, depending on size), cleaned, rinsed, and dried

Salt and black pepper to taste

½ cup (118 mL) white wine vinegar

⅓ cup (57 g) pine nuts

Preheat the oven to 350°F (180°C/gas mark 4).

If the sultanas seem dry, soak them in warm water for a few minutes, then squeeze dry. Oil a large ovenproof skillet and arrange the fish head to tail in a single layer. Season with salt and pepper, splash with vinegar, and sprinkle over the nuts and raisins. Drizzle the remaining oil over the fish. Gently cook on a low flame for 15 minutes, then transfer to the oven for another 15 minutes, or until they are golden brown on top and opaque throughout.

Crespelle con Aneto e Salmone Affumicato
Dill and Spinach Pancakes with Smoked Salmon

*R*ome discovered smoked salmon in the seventies with all the enthusiasm of a city that loves food. In the beginning it occupied a rather insecure place on the Italian menu, coming at the end of a lavish seafood antipasto in Ostia trattorias, served, rather strangely, nestling in the hollow center of rosetti rolls. I remember on one occasion watching bemused as a fur-coated Signora made a whole meal of smoked salmon rosetti, *calling imperiously "Bis" each time she was ready for another. One of the first shops to introduce Rome to salmon, fresh and smoked, was La Corte in Vicolo della Gatta. The salmon was smoked just outside Rome in Licenza, almost next door to the ancient villa of Horace, the Latin poet.*

PANCAKES

3 cups (99 g) spinach
  leaves, cooked and
  squeezed dry

¼ cup (10 g) chopped
  fresh dill

1 egg, beaten

¾ cup (120 g) all-
  purpose (plain) flour

1 cup (237 mL) milk,
  diluted with 1 cup
  (237 mL) of water

———————

4 tablespoons (57 g)
  butter

1 tablespoon (15 mL)
  fresh lemon juice

4 slices smoked salmon

4 sprigs fresh dill, for
  garnish

To make the pancake mixture, purée the spinach, chopped dill, egg, flour, and milk and water in a blender or food processor, then leave at room temperature for at least 1 hour.

Melt half the butter in a large skillet and fry 4 thin pancakes. Leave to cool so that they are easier to handle. When ready to serve, melt the remaining butter and mix in the lemon juice. Cover each pancake with a slice of smoked salmon, roll up, and brush with the butter and lemon juice mixture. Cut in half and decorate with sprigs of dill.

Scorfano in Guazzetto

Scorpion Fish in Tomato Sauce

The great Mediterranean fish rascasse *(in French), or* scorfano, *is used in this recipe, and the sauce can be used to dress a plate of pasta, or diluted and served with the flaked fish to make a robust soup. Other fish or shellfish can be cooked in the same way. I like to make a one-course* scorfano *fish soup, served with crusty bread.*

4 tablespoons (59 mL)
   extra virgin olive oil

2 cloves garlic, finely
   chopped

1 small dried chile
   pepper, crushed

3 plum tomatoes,
   peeled and chopped
   (see page 119)

2 scorpion fish, (large
   enough for 2 people)
   each scaled and cleaned

Salt and black pepper
   to taste

2 tablespoons chopped
   fresh parsley

Light stock (see page
   118), heated to boiling
   (optional)

Heat the oil in a large pan and gently brown the garlic and chile pepper before adding the tomatoes. Simmer for 15 minutes. Season the fish with salt and pepper and place in a close-fitting pan. Pour over the tomatoes, cover, and cook gently for 10 minutes. Remove the fish and fillet it. Add the parsley to the sauce, stir well, and serve with the fish. If you want to serve as a soup, add boiling stock and cook another few minutes.

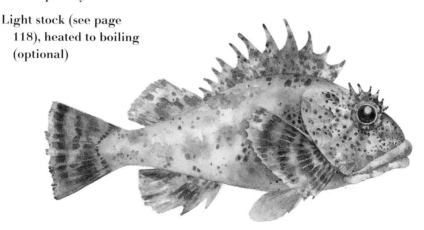

Spigola in Acqua Pazza

Sea Bass Sautéed with Garlic and Chile

This simple recipe, literally *"sea bass in mad water,"* has gained great popularity in Rome although originally it was a Neapolitan fishermen's dish. They would embark with olive oil, garlic, chiles, and a few tomatoes. The least valuable fish caught would be cooked straight from the sea on the hot rims of their acetylene lamps, using seawater *"maddened"* by the garlic and chile.

The recipe is very simple and unbelievably good, but it does need to be cooked at the last minute. I usually cook it between courses, and get the guests to fillet the fish as I bring them to table. On one memorable occasion enough wine had circulated to inspire the men to remove their jackets and have an impromptu competition to see who could fillet the sea bass with most speed and panache. Flushed with success and very pleased with themselves, they turned round to see one of the women already serving her neatly dissected fish. Only attempt to do this dish with good fresh fish, and remember that the small tomatoes should put orange flecks in the translucent sauce, not make an opaque mask. If you prefer to use fish that is already filleted, ask your fishmonger for the carcasses and boil them in lightly salted water for 15 minutes to make the *"mad water."*

2 sea bass, cleaned, or 4 fillets, with the carcasses saved for stock

Salt to taste

¼ cup (59 mL) extra virgin olive oil

2 cloves garlic, chopped

1 small dried chile pepper, crushed

8 tasty cherry tomatoes, slit

1 tablespoon chopped fresh parsley

If using the fillets and carcasses, boil the carcasses in 2 cups salted water for 15 minutes to make "mad water."

In a large shallow pan, heat the oil and add the garlic, chile, and fish fillets or whole fish. Season the fish with salt. Sauté for a few minutes, then pour in 2 cups (473 mL) of the mad water. Add the tomatoes and, using the back of a wooden spoon, squash them against the sides of the pan. Sprinkle in the parsley, cover, and cook gently until the fish are done. (The exact time will depend on the size of the fish.) Carefully remove the fish to avoid breaking, and remove the flesh of the whole fish from the bone. Serve with spoonfuls of the cooking liquid, leaving the tomato skins in the pan.

Spigola con la Salsa di Zucchini

Sea Bass with Zucchini Sauce

Angelo Cabani of Miranda restaurant in Tellaro cooks beautifully light fish dishes with an olive oil and vegetable sauce. His menu always reflects the vegetables in season, and I love to cook this summer dish inspired by his style of cooking.

1 large or 2 smaller sea
   bass, cleaned

Salt and black pepper
   to taste

4 zucchini (courgettes)

8 basil leaves

Juice of 1 lemon

¼ cup (59 mL) extra
   virgin olive oil

Preheat the oven to 350°F (175°C/gas mark 4).

Season the fish with salt and pepper and wrap in lightly oiled aluminum kitchen foil. Bake until cooked to your personal preference. I usually allow 30 minutes.

Coarsely chop 2 of the zucchini. Cut the remaining 2 zucchini into thin slices. Cook the zucchini slices in a little boiling salted water, drain, and set aside. Cook the remaining zucchini in 1 cup (237 mL) boiling water. In a blender or food processor, purée the zucchini with a little of their cooking liquid, the basil, and lemon juice. Emulsify the mixture with the olive oil in a blender. Season to taste. Fillet the fish and serve on a bed of the zucchini sauce, decorated with the zucchini slices.

Pesce al Forno con Patate, Pomodorini, e Olive

Fish Baked with Potatoes, Tomatoes, and Black Olives

We love to eat this fish dish for Sunday lunch, when the first days of spring are sunny but cool enough not to make turning on the oven the act of a masochist.

4 tablespoons (59 mL)
  extra virgin olive oil

1 large sea bass, cleaned
  and scaled

1 small onion, finely sliced

4 medium potatoes,
  peeled and thinly sliced

½ cup (114 g) black olives

8 small cherry tomatoes

Salt and black pepper
  to taste

Fresh rosemary leaves
  to taste

Preheat the oven to 375°F (190°C/gas mark 5).

Pour half the oil into a large, shallow baking dish and place the fish on top. Surround with the sliced onion and potatoes. Arrange the olives and tomatoes on top. Add seasoning and sprinkle the rosemary leaves over the fish and vegetables. Drizzle on the remaining oil and bake for about 40 minutes.

Trota Salmonata ai Finocchi
Coho with Fennel

*R*ainbow trout have long been a Roman delicacy, but coho, or farmed salmon trout, were introduced in the last decade. They can now be found in most Roman markets, and since they are a "modern" fish, they are usually served the modern way, filleted.

2 fennel bulbs, cleaned, trimmed, and sliced

2 tablespoons (30 mL) extra virgin olive oil

2 coho (or pink trout), weighing about 18 ounces (510 g) each, cleaned and filleted

Juice of 1 lemon

Salt and black pepper to taste

1 sprig wild fennel, dill, or fronds from cultivated fennel, chopped

½ teaspoon chopped fresh rosemary leaves

Preheat the oven to 400°F (200°C/gas mark 6).

Cook the fennel for 5 minutes in lightly salted boiling water. Drain.

Brush an oval or rectangular oven dish with olive oil and arrange the fish fillets in a single layer. Brush the fish with a little olive oil and dribble on the lemon juice. Season with salt and pepper. Cover the fish with the drained slices of fennel, topped with the chopped herbs. Dribble on the remaining olive oil and a little black pepper and bake for 10 minutes.

Trota Farcita al Vino Rosso

Stuffed Trout in Red Wine

Rome has many neighboring lakes and rivers supplying freshwater fish. Traditionally, fish is cooked very simply with olive oil and rosemary, then served whole, complete with head and tail. Until a few years ago it was customary for the restaurants to show the raw fish to the customers who carefully inspected the gills and eyes to determine the freshness of the fish. This recipe is a "new" variation, and the stuffing and red wine make it suitable for colder weather.

4 whole trout, about 8 ounces (227 g) each

1 tablespoon (7g) fresh bread crumbs

4 shallots, finely chopped

2 tablespoons finely chopped fresh parsley

8 ounces (227 g) mushrooms, chopped

1 clove garlic, finely chopped

2 tablespoons (30 mL) extra virgin olive oil

Salt and black pepper to taste

Flour for dusting

1 carrot, scraped and chopped

1 stalk celery, scraped and chopped

1 bottle dry red wine

Clean, rinse, and pat dry the trout.

Mix together the bread crumbs, half the shallots, half the parsley, the mushrooms, garlic, and 1 tablespoon (15 mL) of the olive oil. Season with salt and pepper. Season the inside of the trout, then stuff with the mushroom mixture. Dust the trout with flour and put to one side.

In a large flat pan that will contain the 4 trout, heat the remaining 1 tablespoon (15 mL) olive oil and gently fry the remaining shallots with the carrot and celery. Pour in a little wine and lift the fish into the pan. Cover with wine and cook gently for 15 minutes.

Remove carefully to avoid breaking the fish and arrange on a serving dish, with the remaining parsley sprinkled on top. Keep the fish warm while puréeing the cooking vegetables and sauce. If the sauce seems too thin, reduce it over high heat. Serve the fish and the sauce separately.

Filetti di Rombo al Cartoccio

Turbot Fillets Baked in Paper

In Rome, turbot, or rombo, is one of the most prized fish. The Roman emperor Domitian, when presented with a superb rombo, *called a council meeting to decide how to cook it, and ordered a special plate to be made on which to display the prized specimen.*

When I prepare this recipe I often put some artichoke purée in the center of the fillets, but my friends joke that, given the chance, I would eat artichokes for every course. They are quite right. At the restaurant Evangelista at the beginning of the season I started my dinner with the house specialty, roasted artichokes hammered flat, continued with artichoke soup, and finished with a layered baked pie made with potatoes and artichokes. Alas, there was no artichoke dessert!

4 large or 8 small fillets turbot or sole, 1 pound (454 g) total, skinned

Salt and black pepper to taste

1 clove garlic, minced

2 tablespoons chopped fresh parsley

¾ cup (198 g) plus 2 tablespoons (28 g) butter

4 young scallions (spring onions), finely chopped

1 small dried chile pepper, crushed

Grated zest of 1 lemon

Preheat the oven to 350°F (180°C/gas mark 4).

Season the fish fillets with salt and pepper, sprinkle on the garlic and parsley, and roll up tightly. Place each roll in the center of a square of baking parchment, fold in the sides, and roll up. Tie with kitchen string. Arrange the parcels in a baking dish and bake for 15 minutes.

Just before serving, melt the butter gently in a small saucepan, adding the scallions, chile, and zest. Do not let the butter change color. Remove the fish from the oven, discard the string and paper, and serve with the butter sauce.

Filetti di Rombo al Basilico

Turbot Fillets with Basil and Olive Oil Dressing

When Rome is really hot in June or July, meat seems less attractive than it does in the winter, and these delicate fish dishes are always very inviting. In Testaccio market Rita always has beautiful bunches of fresh basil, nestling under damp sacking to keep fresh even in the extreme heat.

1 clove garlic

2 turbot, each enough for
  2 people, cleaned

FISH STOCK

Reserved fish carcasses

1 small onion, coarsely
  chopped

1 stalk celery, coarsely
  chopped

1 small carrot, scraped
  and coarsely chopped

1 cup (237 mL) dry white
  wine

———————

1 bunch basil, stemmed

½ cup (118 mL) extra
  virgin olive oil

Salt and black pepper
  to taste

4 sprigs basil for garnish

4 cherry tomatoes for
  garnish

Blanch the garlic by covering it with cold water and bringing it to a boil. Discard the water and repeat the process twice more. Fillet and skin the fish and reserve the carcasses for stock.

To make the fish stock, put the fish carcasses, onion, celery, and carrot to stew with the white wine and add just enough lightly salted water to cover the fish. Boil slowly until the liquid is reduced by half. Pour through a strainer and allow to cool. This can be prepared several hours in advance.

At least 1 hour before you want to serve the fish, plunge the basil leaves into boiling water, remove and drain thoroughly, and wrap in a kitchen towel. In a blender or food processor, blend the oil and, as it begins to emulsify, add the basil leaves, garlic, and 1 cup (237 mL) fish stock. Allow to stand at room temperature and adjust seasoning before using.

When ready to eat, lightly steam the fish fillets over boiling water, or until cooked. Serve with the basil dressing, decorated with a sprig of fresh basil and a cherry tomato.

Zuppa di Pesce con la Crosta
Fish Soup with Pastry Lids

*M*any of the great Mediterranean fish soups do not transfer well to other regions of the world, but this soup can be prepared with any fresh good-flavored fish. When the soup is eaten the pastry lid should be broken into the soup in stages, so that the pastry remains crisp.

PASTRY

2 cups (298 g) all-purpose (plain) flour

Pinch of salt

⅔ cup (155 g) butter

Water

---

1 large white fish, such as gray mullet, weighing about 2 pounds (907 g), or 2 smaller white fish, cleaned

STOCK

Reserved fish carcass

1 small onion, chopped

1 stalk celery, chopped

1 carrot, chopped

Salt and black pepper to taste

1 cup (237 mL) dry white wine

To make the pastry, combine the flour and salt. Rub the butter into the flour, then add enough water to make a normal shortcrust pastry. Roll into a ball, wrap in cooking foil, and refrigerate for at least 30 minutes.

Fillet the fish, reserving the carcass. To make the stock, put the fish carcass into a pan with the onion, celery, and carrot and 4 cups (946 mL) water. Bring to a boil, then add salt and white wine. Cook gently for 30 minutes, then strain and set aside.

3 tablespoons (44 mL)
    extra virgin olive oil

1 anchovy fillet

1 small dried chile
    pepper, crushed

2 cloves garlic, chopped

6 ripe tomatoes, peeled
    and chopped

7 ounces (198 g) shrimp
    (prawns), cleaned and
    deveined

2 tablespoons fresh
    chopped parsley

1 egg

1 tablespoon (15 mL) milk

In a large pan, heat the oil and cook the anchovy, chile, and garlic until the garlic begins to change color. Put in the tomatoes and after 5 minutes pour in the stock. Bring back to a boil and put in the fish fillets, shrimp, and parsley. Cook for another 5 minutes, adjust seasoning, and allow to cool.

Preheat the oven to 350°F (180°C/gas mark 4).

Break the fish into small pieces and ladle the soup into 4 ovenproof soup bowls. In a small bowl, beat the egg and milk together. Roll out the pastry and cut out 4 large circles and 4 long strips. Place a strip around the top of each soup bowl, brush with the egg mixture, and cover with the large circles, pressing the seams firmly to seal. Brush the tops with the egg mixture and bake until golden brown, about 15 minutes.

Fritto di Mare

Fried Small Fish

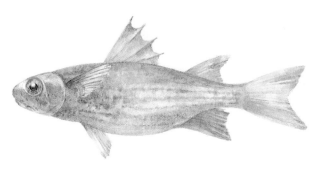

In old Roman cooking the fritto di mare *was very different from the floured squid and shrimp popular today at trattorias in Ostia and Fiumicino. The older version uses very small fresh fish, and although this recipe causes the hot oil to sputter quite alarmingly, the taste is so good it is worth the inconvenience.*

Olive oil for frying

4 small red mullet,
   cleaned but left whole

4 small cod, cleaned but
   left whole

4 small sole, cleaned but
   left whole

1 clove garlic, finely
   chopped

1 tablespoon chopped
   fresh parsley

Salt to taste

1 lemon, cut in wedges for
   garnish

In a large pan, heat the oil. Wash the fish and, without drying them, plunge them into hot oil. Turn them around until they are crisp and golden brown, then add the garlic and parsley to the oil. Using a slotted spoon, transfer the fish to paper towels (kitchen paper). Salt and serve straight away with lemon wedges.

Filetti di Baccalà Fritti

Fried Salt Cod

This is a great Roman specialty, and for a typical antipasto the fried fillets are served with an artichoke, Jewish style, and a zucchini blossom fried in batter. Wickedly sinful!

In Largo dei Librari there is a simple "fry shop" that serves crisp, golden fillets of baccalà. Filettaro a Santa Barbara is only open in the evening, and for little more than 10,000 lire you can enjoy the fried fish and a glass of white Castelli wine.

¾ cup (99 g) all-purpose (plain) flour

Pinch of salt

3 cups (710 mL) water

14 ounces (397 g) salt cod, soaked for 48 hours in cold water

2 egg whites, whipped to stiff peaks

Olive oil for deep-frying

Mix the flour and salt with the 3 cups of water to make a thick batter. Leave to stand for at least 1 hour. Drain the fish and cut it into thin strips. When ready to fry, fold the whipped egg whites into the batter, dip in the fish, and fry on both sides until crisp and golden brown. Serve at once.

Mazzancolle al Coccio
Shrimp Cooked in Wine

*T*he Roman name comes from the flat earthenware dish in which the shrimp (prawns) are cooked. It is possible to use any flat pan, but I like to use a shallow terra-cotta two-handled dish on top of the stove, using a heat deflector (diffuser) to avoid breakage. When I carry the pan directly to the table, the shrimp (prawns) are still sizzling in the oil and white wine. You can also use small individual pans if desired. Although gingerroot does not appear in traditional Italian recipes, it is now sold in all the markets, and it is often used to add an extra dimension to shellfish.

2 pounds (907 g) large shrimp (prawns), shelled and deveined

3 cloves garlic, cut into fine slivers

1 small piece peeled gingerroot, cut into slivers

4 tablespoons (59 mL) extra virgin olive oil

Juice of 1 lemon

Salt to taste

1 tablespoon chopped fresh parsley

1 small dried chile pepper, chopped

1 cup (237 mL) dry white wine

Rinse the shrimp and pat dry with paper towels (kitchen paper). Make 3 or 4 incisions in the back of the shrimp where you removed the vein, and spike with alternate slivers of garlic and gingerroot. Pour over half the oil, the lemon juice, a little salt, the parsley, and the chile pepper. Scatter any leftover pieces of garlic and gingerroot over the top. When ready to serve, heat the remaining oil and add the shrimp and their mixture. Cook quickly on each side, splash over the wine, shake the pan, and allow the wine to reduce. Serve at once with good fresh bread to mop up the juices.

Cozze Gratinate

Baked Mussels

In Trastevere, the area across the river Tiber, there are many trattorias, and although tourist menus and fashionable quirks have eroded some traditional values and destroyed several good old eating places, in the side streets it is sometimes still possible to eat "alla romana," with friendly, good-natured waiters bustling about to satisfy their "regulars." This is a typical Friday starter that converted me to eating mussels when I first came to Rome. A glass of cold Castelli white wine completes the feast.

2 tablespoons (28 g) dried
  bread crumbs

2 cloves garlic, minced

2 tablespoons chopped
  fresh parsley

Grated zest of 1 lemon

Salt and black pepper
  to taste

2 pounds (907 g) mussels
  in their shells, scrubbed
  and debearded

2 tablespoons (30 mL)
  extra virgin olive oil

Preheat the oven to 350°F (175°C/gas mark 4).

Mix together the bread crumbs, garlic, parsley, and zest. Season with salt and pepper. Place the mussels in a large saucepan with 1 tablespoon water, over high heat. Discard any mussels that fail to open.

Remove the mussels from the shell. Break the shells in half. Place 2 mussels in one half shell and sprinkle some bread mixture over the top. Prepare all the mussels in this way and arrange on a baking tray. Drizzle the olive oil over the stuffed mussels. Bake for about 5 minutes, or until golden brown. Serve hot.

POULTRY
& MEAT

Traditionally, Romans have always preferred young milk-fed lamb or kid for special occasions, using pork and home-cured pork products as a tasty but less expensive alternative. Beef and veal used not to be available in Rome, but today they are sold all through the year, while pork and lamb disappear during the summer months. This probably dates back to the time when the animals were not killed until the beginning of winter when the fodder ran out. Until well after World War II, most families could afford to eat meat only once a week, and recipes evolved to make the most of cheaper cuts. Good-quality meat has always been cooked very simply with a little seasoning and herbs to enhance the natural flavor, and today in the city the griddle or frying pan replaces the wood fire. Most Roman cooking is done on top of the stove, and grills and ovens are seldom used. Rich masking sauces do not appear in Roman meat and poultry dishes, and the tougher cuts are cooked slowly with fresh herbs and vegetables. Olive oil has gradually replaced the more traditional lard, which was used when most families kept a pig.

In 1890 a modern slaughterhouse was opened in the Testaccio area of Rome to feed the rapidly growing capital of the new Italy. Offal, trotters, tails, heads, and intestines had little commercial value, and this *quinto quarto*, or fifth quarter of the animal, was paid out as part of their wages to the workers. Tasty dishes using these less-than-promising ingredients became very popular, and today Romans like to eat in the trattorias around Testaccio, which, even though the slaughterhouse has closed, continue to serve *coda alla caccinara* (oxtail), and *pajata* (veal small intestines).

Roman butchers are gradually starting to prepare ready-made meatballs, meat loaf, and *involtini* (meat rolls). Until a few years ago they were unable to sell a steak if it had been already cut from the large side of beef, and the customer selected the meat and waited for it to be cut, sawn, and trimmed. Most people rely on very thin slices, or *fettine*, of beef or veal. Chicken and turkey breasts are treated in the same way, and you have to be very quick to prevent the butcher automatically cutting a chicken breast into slivers.

Involtini di Pollo e Mozzarella
Chicken and Mozzarella Rolls

This is a good dish for summer when more substantial fare is unthinkable. During the heat of the day the city seems deserted as shutters close rank against the sun, and even the traffic is muted. But when the cooler evening air starts to move over the city Rome comes back to life. The piazzas buzz in a party mood and every café and pizzeria sprouts tables and chairs in all directions. Wherever you look, a convivial throng is talking, laughing, and eating, even if it is only a gelato.

8 small slices boneless,
   skinless chicken breast

Salt and black pepper
   to taste

8 thin slices mozzarella

8 leaves basil

2 tablespoons (28 g)
   butter

1 tablespoon (15 mL)
   extra virgin olive oil

½ cup (118 mL) dry white
   wine

Beat the chicken slices flat with a mallet. Season the chicken slices with salt and pepper and place a slice of mozzarella and a basil leaf on top of each. Roll up and fasten with a toothpick. In a large pan, heat the butter and oil and gently brown the chicken rolls. Splash over the wine, cover, and gently simmer for about 20 minutes, or until cooked. Remove the toothpicks and serve with the pan juices.

Pollo alla Romana

Chicken with Tomatoes and Green Peppers

*T*his dish is often served with red bell peppers (capsicums) that give a sweet flavor to the chicken, but green peppers with their distinctive bitter tang are more authentic. The whole chicken should be used to gain flavor, and if you substitute all breast meat you will get a much blander taste.

¼ cup (59 mL) olive oil

2 ounces (57 g) pancetta or bacon, chopped (optional)

2 cloves garlic, minced

1 chicken, cut into serving pieces

½ cup (118 mL) dry white wine, preferably Frascati

18 ounces (510 g) full-flavored red tomatoes or canned Italian tomatoes

3 green bell peppers (capsicums), seeds and fibers removed, cut in strips

Salt and black pepper to taste

In a large pan, heat the oil. (If you are using the pancetta, gently stew it in the oil until the fat runs out.) Now add the garlic and chicken pieces and cook until they begin to change color. Pour in the wine and cook over low heat for 5 minutes. Stir in the tomatoes and peppers, season with salt and pepper, and cook gently for about 45 minutes.

Pollo al Limone e Balsamico
Chicken with Lemon and Balsamic Vinegar

Balsamic *vinegar originated in Modena and Reggio Emilia centuries ago. Today local families still make balsamic vinegar in the traditional way, aging the vinegar in a series of casks made of five different woods, each contributing its own flavor to the vinegar. Some casks still in use date back to the sixteenth century, and the old casks have been skillfully enclosed inside new ones to prevent the precious substance oozing away. When Lucrezia Borgia was married to the Duke of Modena, she inhaled the fumes from balsamic vinegar to help her during childbirth. In the past Modena used this precious commodity to negotiate treaties with foreign rulers such as Bismarck and Catherine the Great of Russia, and today local producers deal with specialist stores all over the world. In Rome traditionally produced* balsamico *can be found in food shops in Via del Croce, or wine merchants like Trimani. The small bottles bearing the seal of approval from the "Consorzio" at Modena cost a duke's ransom, but it is possible to find younger, less expensive vinegars. Factory-produced balsamic vinegar is a very, very pale imitation of the real thing.*

4 boneless, skinless
  chicken breast halves

Salt and black pepper
  to taste

1 shallot, finely chopped

2 tablespoons (30 mL)
  extra virgin olive oil

¼ cup (59 mL) light stock
  (see page 118)

Finely shredded zest and
  juice of 2 lemons

1 tablespoon (15 mL)
  honey (optional)

1 tablespoon (15 mL)
  balsamic vinegar

Season the chicken fillets with salt and pepper to taste. In a large pan, heat the shallot and the oil and gently brown the chicken fillets on each side. Add the stock, lemon zest, lemon juice, and honey if used. Simmer until the chicken is cooked through.

Remove to a serving dish and dribble the balsamic vinegar over the chicken. Wait 1 minute before pouring the sauce over the top.

Petto di Tacchino con Funghi

Sliced Turkey Breast with Mushrooms

This makes a quick, easy lunch and I find everyone loves it. It goes very well with Sformato di Patate (page 63).

1 boneless, skinless turkey
   breast half

Flour for dusting

3 tablespoons (44 mL)
   extra virgin olive oil

1 small onion, finely
   chopped

14 ounces (397 g) cremini
   (field) or white mush-
   rooms, sliced

Salt and black pepper
   to taste

1 cup (237 mL) dry white
   wine

1 tablespoon chopped
   fresh parsley

Cut the turkey breast into 8 horizontal slices. Dust the turkey slices with flour and set aside. In a large pan, heat half the oil and gently cook the onion until soft. Add the mushrooms, season with salt and pepper, and simmer for 10 minutes. Heat the remaining oil and cook the floured turkey slices in batches until golden brown on both sides. Return to the pan, pour over the wine, let it bubble for a few minutes, then stir in the parsley. Serve with the mushrooms spooned over the top.

Garofolato e Sugo d'Umido
Beef Pot Roast with Meat Sauce

This great Roman dish is named after the cloves, chiodi di garofani, *with which the meat is spiked. In the past the rich sauce known as* sugo di umido *was used to dress pasta, and the meat was served on another occasion in typical* cucina povera *tradition. Today the meat and sauce are usually served together, and the extra sauce is mopped up with coarse bread,* pane casereccia. *The half slices of oval bread look like the heel of a flat shoe, or* scarpetta, *and when you wipe your plate with bread it is known as* fare la scarpetta *(to make the shoe).*

2 pounds (907 g) beef, usually top round (topside)

2 ounces (57 g) prosciutto, cut into thin strips

1 clove garlic, cut into slivers

6 cloves

Salt and black pepper to taste

2 tablespoons (30 mL) extra virgin olive oil

2 teaspoons coarsely chopped fresh marjoram or 1 tablespoon chopped parsley

1 onion, chopped

1 carrot, scraped and chopped

1 stalk celery, scraped and chopped

2 tomatoes, peeled and chopped (see page 119)

1 cup (237 mL) dry red wine

Make deep holes in the meat and lard it with strips of prosciutto using a larding needle if available. If not, use a skewer to push in the strips of prosciutto. Make a row of incisions along the length of the meat and insert slivers of garlic alternated with cloves. Season the meat with salt and pepper.

In a Dutch oven just large enough to hold the meat and vegetables, heat the oil and brown the meat on all sides. Surround the meat with the marjoram and vegetables. Pour over the wine and let half evaporate before adding enough boiling water to just cover the meat. Cover the pan and cook slowly for about 1½ to 2 hours.

Remove the meat, keep warm, and purée the vegetables and cooking liquid to produce a dense, rich brown sauce. Cut the meat in thick slices and spoon over the sauce.

Manzo Brasato in Vino Rosso

Beef in Red Wine

Good beef is not a traditional Roman ingredient and not every Roman butcher knows his beef. I usually buy mine from La Fiorentina in Campo de' Fiori, where Scottish beef competes with the delectable Tuscan chianana. These cattle were originally raised by the Etruscans, and at a later date the Romans, to sacrifice to their gods. Judging by the eager crowd thronging La Fiorentina, present-day mortals are just as discerning. I like to use a full-bodied red wine like Cabernet Sauvignon. This dish should be served with potatoes or polenta.

2 pounds (907 g) lean beef

2 onions

1 stalk celery, scraped and coarsely chopped

1 carrot, scraped and thickly sliced

1 bay leaf

2 cloves

1½-inch (3-cm) piece stick cinnamon

6 black peppercorns

1 bottle dry red wine

Flour for dusting

Salt to taste

2 tablespoons (30 mL) extra virgin olive oil

1 potato, peeled and sliced

1 tomato, peeled and chopped (see page 119)

4 leaves sage

1 sprig rosemary

Put the meat into a close-fitting glass or china bowl. Coarsely chop one onion. Add the onion, celery, carrot, bay leaf, cloves, cinnamon, and peppercorns to the bowl, and cover with red wine. Leave to marinate overnight.

When ready to cook, lift out the meat from the marinade and drain. Pat dry with paper towels (kitchen paper) and dust lightly with flour and salt. Reserve the marinade.

Finely chop the other onion. In a heavy pot that will just contain the meat, heat the oil and gently fry the chopped onion until soft. Add the meat and lightly brown on all sides.

Strain the marinade and set aside. Chop the marinade vegetables before adding them to the meat. Stir in the potato, tomato, strained marinade, sage, and rosemary. Cover and cook slowly for about 90 minutes. Lift out the meat. Remove and discard the rosemary and bay leaf. In a blender or food processor, purée the vegetables and their sauce. Check the seasoning. The meat should be cut in thick slices and served with potatoes or polenta.

Braciolette d' Abbacchio Scottadito

Grilled Lamb Chops

*R*omans are proud of their very young lamb, and here the tiny chops are
served straight from the grill, so hot they burn your fingers, as you hold
them in your hand and nibble the tender meat.

**2 small lamb chops, per
serving**

Flour for dusting

**Salt and black pepper
to taste**

**Rosemary leaves
(optional)**

**1 tablespoon (15 mL)
olive oil**

Hammer the lamb chops flat, then dust
them with flour and salt and pepper. A little
rosemary can be sprinkled on top. Brush with
oil and cook in a heavy pan or on a grill until
they are crisp and golden brown.

Abbacchio alla Cacciatora

Lamb, Hunter Style

There are many, many variations of cacciatora recipes, and no one has ever explained the origin of this dish to my satisfaction. Most recipes contain vinegar and it has been said this was to preserve the meat so that the hunters could take it with them when they set out to hunt. I find this strange since it would seem more normal for the hunters to hunt for their food, and barbecue it on the spot! However, whatever the origin of the name, the finished dish is very tasty, and perfect for cold weather. This recipe is also used for chicken.

1 leg of lamb, about 2
   pounds (907 g), chopped
   into pieces weighing
   about 1½ ounces (42 g)

Salt and black pepper
   to taste

4 tablespoons (59 mL)
   olive oil

2 cloves garlic, finely
   chopped

2 sage leaves

2 teaspoons chopped fresh
   rosemary

1 tablespoon flour

½ cup (118 mL) white
   wine vinegar, diluted
   with ½ cup (118 mL)
   water

1 cup (237 mL) water

2 anchovy fillets

Season the lamb with salt and pepper. In a large pan, heat 3 tablespoons (44 mL) of the oil and quickly brown the seasoned lamb on all sides. Sprinkle over the garlic, sage, and rosemary, and stir around the pan. Sprinkle the flour over the lamb, stir round the pan, and pour in the vinegar and water. Stir for a few minutes, add the 1 cup (237 mL) of water, cover, and simmer. Add more water if it becomes too dry.

In a small pan, heat the remaining oil and gently stew the anchovies, pushing them with the back of a wooden spoon until they seem to melt into the oil. Add a little of the lamb cooking liquid. When the lamb is tender, remove from the pan with a slotted spoon and stir the anchovy mixture into the cooking liquid. Strain the thick, dark sauce, check the seasoning, pour the sauce over the meat, and serve.

Arista al Finocchio

Roast Pork with Fennel

The cut of meat traditionally used for this dish is the boned best end of the neck, but today loin is normally used. It is believed that during the Ecumenical Council in Florence in 1430, the Greek bishops ate roast pork and with one voice declared, "It is the best (áristos). The meat was promptly christened arista, and the name is now used throughout Italy.

Wild fennel is used to give a pungent flavor to pork, but the green leafy fronds from cultivated fennel bulbs can be substituted if wild fennel is not available.

1 teaspoon coarse salt

6 black peppercorns

2 cloves garlic, finely chopped

2 ounces (57 g) wild fennel or fronds from cultivated fennel

¼ teaspoon freshly grated nutmeg

2 pounds (907 g) boned pork loin

2 tablespoons (30 mL) extra virgin olive oil

1 cup (237 mL) dry white wine

4 fennel bulbs, trimmed and divided into segments

Preheat the oven to 350°F (180°C/gas mark 4).

Crush the salt and pepper and chop together with the garlic and fennel greenery. Grate on nutmeg. Rub this mixture into the pork and dribble the olive oil over the top. Place in a roasting pan just large enough for the pork and, at a later stage, the fennel.

Roast for about 1 hour, gradually adding the white wine and basting frequently with the cooking juices. Boil the fennel in lightly salted water for 5 minutes. Drain and arrange round the pork for the last 20 minutes' roasting time. When the meat is cooked, remove from the pan. Allow to stand for a few minutes before carving. Serve with the fennel and pan juices.

Spezzatino di Cinghiale
Wild Boar Casserole

North of Rome, along the Via Cassia, you find the small historic town of Campagnano. Many of the local inhabitants still grow all their own vegetables and make their own olive oil and wine. In autumn they prepare this succulent casserole, and if you are lucky enough to be invited for Sunday lunch, with all the trimmings, you will not be allowed up from the table until it is quite dark. Serve with polenta, white beans, or puréed chestnuts.

2 pounds (907 g) wild boar, or pork, cut into small pieces

1 clove garlic, chopped

4 shallots, chopped

2 carrots, scraped and chopped

2 stalks celery, scraped and chopped

3 or 4 peppercorns

¾ cup plus 2 tablespoons (200 mL) dry red wine

3 tablespoons (44 mL) extra virgin olive oil

2 ounces (57 g) pancetta or bacon, diced

Salt and black pepper to taste

2 apples, peeled, cored, and sliced

Put the meat in a close-fitting glass or china bowl together with the garlic, shallots, and half the chopped vegetables. Add the peppercorns and pour over the wine. Cover and refrigerate for 12 hours, stirring from time to time.

In a large pan, heat the oil, add the pancetta and the remaining chopped vegetables, and cook gently for a few minutes. With a slotted spoon, remove the meat from the marinade, drain, and pat dry. Strain and reserve the marinade.

Brown the pieces of meat in the pancetta mixture, then pour in the strained marinade. Add salt and pepper, cover, and simmer for 1½ to 2 hours, or until tender.

Thirty minutes before the meat is cooked, add the apple slices to the stew. Remove the meat. In a blender or food processor, purée the apples and cooking liquid to make a dense sauce. Pour over the meat and serve.

Cotecchino alla Regina Coeli
Cotecchino Sausage and Veal Rolls

Several years ago while I was lunching in London at a fashionable Italian restaurant I noticed that one of the pasta dishes was called Pasta Regina Coeli. When I asked the waiter for an explanation of the name, I was told that the chef had named it after a place where he had spent many years. That is the name of Rome's main prison (Queen of the Heavens), and they were a little taken back at my laughter since they had felt their joke was quite safe in London. This recipe, given to me by Romano, a buon gustaio *Roman taxi driver, deserves the name since the cotecchino is tied up in its meat prison. Romano prepares this for December 24, when he takes most of the day off.*

1 small cotecchino
   sausage

1 flat piece of lean veal,
   about 18 ounces (510 g),
   beaten flat

Salt and black pepper
   to taste

2 tablespoons (30 mL)
   extra virgin olive oil

1 large onion, finely
   chopped

1 stalk celery, chopped

2 tablespoons (30 mL) dry
   Marsala or white wine

1 bay leaf

1 tablespoon chopped
   fresh parsley

8 small whole onions

4 carrots, thinly sliced

Prick the sausage in several places, and place in a large pan. Cover with cold water and bring to a boil. Lower heat and simmer for 10 minutes, then discard the water. Allow the sausage to cool enough to handle, and peel it. Lay the veal out flat and season it with salt and pepper. Arrange the sausage in the middle of the veal, then roll up the meat and tie in several places with kitchen string.

In a large pan, heat the oil and cook the onion and celery until soft. Gently place the meat in the pan and brown on all sides. Pour over the wine, add the bay leaf and parsley, and simmer for 1 hour, adding a little water from time to time if necessary. Add the small onions, carrots, and a little water, then simmer for another 30 minutes. Check the seasoning and lift out the meat. Remove and discard the bay leaf. Remove the string, cut open the sides, and cut the roll into thick slices. Serve with the vegetables and cooking juices.

Polpettone alla Flavia
Flavia's Meat Loaf

*A*lthough this could be called good old meat loaf masquerading as something exotic, the disguise is superlative! Every region in Italy has their version of polpettone, *and in Rome every family has their favorite recipe. My friend Flavia makes a very good* polpettone, *which is tasty and moist. They can tend to be rather dry. Her secret is to add some tomato sauce to the meat mixture, and omit the grated Parmesan.*

1¾ pounds (794 g) ground (minced) beef

1 cup (57 g) fresh bread crumbs

2 cloves garlic, finely chopped

2 teaspoons ground cumin

1 tablespoon chopped fresh parsley

1 small onion, finely chopped

1 egg, beaten

2 cups (473 mL) hot fresh tomato sauce (see page 118) plus additional for serving

Salt and black pepper to taste

Extra virgin olive oil for brushing

Preheat the oven to 350°F (180°C/gas mark 4).

Mix together the beef, bread crumbs, garlic, cumin, parsley, onion, egg, tomato sauce, salt, and pepper, using a food processor if preferred. Mold the mixture into the shape of a large sausage, brush with olive oil, and place in an oven dish. Cover with aluminum (kitchen) foil. Bake for 1 hour, then remove the foil and brown for another 15 minutes. Serve in thick slices with hot fresh tomato sauce on the side.

Saltimbocca alla Romana

Veal with Ham and Sage

In this recipe the hidden sage leaves are said to make the meat "jump in the mouth" (saltimbocca). It is a very popular dish, quickly prepared at home, and found on the menu in every trattoria.

8 lean veal scaloppine, about 18 ounces (510 g) total

Salt and black pepper to taste

4 thin slices of prosciutto

8 sage leaves

4 tablespoons (57 g) butter

¼ cup (59 mL) dry white wine

1 tablespoon (15 mL) hot water

Season the scaloppine with salt and pepper. Cut each slice of prosciutto in half. Place a sage leaf, then half a slice of prosciutto, on top of each veal slice, using a wooden toothpick to skewer them together.

In a large pan, melt the butter and gently brown the veal, turning the slices over so that the prosciutto side is briefly in contact with the hot butter. After a few minutes pour over the wine and tilt the pan so that the juices amalgamate. Carefully remove the veal and arrange on a serving plate. Return the pan to the heat and stir in the hot water. Spoon the sauce over the veal slices and serve.

Polpettine di Vitello e Ricotta

Veal and Ricotta Meatballs

I learned to make these light, fluffy meatballs from Benedetta Vitali. They are usually served in a fresh tomato sauce.

9 ounces (255 g) finely ground (minced) veal

1 cup plus 2 tablespoons (255 g) ricotta, drained for an hour

1 egg, beaten

½ cup (57 g) freshly grated Parmesan cheese

A little grated nutmeg

Salt and black pepper to taste

Flour for dusting

Olive oil for frying

2 cups (473 mL) fresh hot tomato sauce (see page 118)

Basil leaves for garnish

In a food processor, blend together the meat, ricotta, egg, Parmesan, nutmeg, salt, and pepper. With wet hands, shape the mixture into small balls and lightly dust with flour. In a large pan, heat the oil and fry the balls a few at a time until they are golden brown all over. Lift out with a slotted spoon and keep warm. Serve with very hot tomato sauce, and garnish with basil leaves.

Piccatine al Limone

Veal Scallops with Lemon

This simple light dish is a firm favorite in my family, and my grandson asks for it at home and in Italian restaurants with the same stubborn determination shown by his mother at his age! The veal can be replaced with thin slices of chicken or turkey breast if desired.

18 ounces (510 g) veal fillet, cut into thin slices

Salt and black pepper to taste

Flour for dusting

4 tablespoons (59 mL/ 57 g) extra virgin olive oil or butter

3 tablespoons (44 mL) fresh lemon juice

1 tablespoon chopped fresh parsley

Season the meat with salt and pepper and dust lightly with flour. In a large pan, heat the oil or butter. Gently cook the veal slices in batches for 2 or 3 minutes on each side. Remove from the pan and arrange, slightly overlapping, on a serving plate. Stir the lemon juice and parsley into the pan juices, heat through, and pour over the meat.

Girello di Vitello e Carciofi al Vino Bianco

Veal and Artichokes Cooked in White Wine

This is an easy dish that can be served happily at family meals or dinner parties. If you are not serving potatoes, have plenty of good crusty bread for the lovely sauce.

1¾ pounds (794 g) lean veal, preferably top round (topside)

Salt and black pepper to taste

Flour for dusting

2 tablespoons (30 mL) extra virgin olive oil

1 onion, chopped

1 bottle dry white wine

2 sprigs mint tied together with string

6 artichokes, trimmed and cut into wedges (see page 119)

4 potatoes, peeled and sliced (optional)

1 tablespoon chopped fresh mint

Cut the veal into slices about ⅝ inch (1.5 cm) thick, season with salt and pepper, and dust with flour. In a large pan, heat the oil and cook the onion until soft. Add the meat and gently seal both sides without letting them brown. Pour over the wine and add the sprigs of mint, tied with cotton string so that they can be discarded before serving. Cover and simmer gently for 30 minutes.

Add the artichokes and the potatoes if desired. Stew for another 25 minutes. Adjust the seasoning and remove the mint sprigs. The meat should be very tender. Just before serving, add the fresh mint, check the seasoning, and serve.

Involtini di Carne e Carciofi

Meat and Artichoke Rolls

I learned this recipe many years ago from Rome's historic restaurant Checcini dal 1887 in Testaccio. Over the years, like all cooks, I have gradually strayed from their original recipe and changed the proportions to suit our own taste, but there are always many variations on a theme in Italian cooking.

3 tablespoons (44 mL)
  extra virgin olive oil

1 onion, finely chopped

4 artichokes, trimmed and
  sliced (see page 119)

1 potato, peeled and
  thinly sliced

1 tablespoon chopped
  fresh parsley

½ cup (118 mL) dry white
  wine

Salt and black pepper
  to taste

Light stock (see page
  118), heated to boiling

8 veal scallops, or
  thin slices of chicken
  or turkey breast,
  beaten flat

8 small slices prosciutto

In a large pan, heat half the oil and gently fry the onion until soft. Stir in the artichokes and potato, then after a few minutes the parsley, wine, salt, and pepper. Add a little boiling stock. Cover and simmer until the vegetables are cooked. Drain, reserving the cooking liquid, and purée in a blender or food processor.

Season the meat and place a small piece of prosciutto on top of each slice. Spoon some vegetable purée on one end. Roll up to form a small cylinder and tie with kitchen string. Make all the rolls in the same way. Heat the remaining oil and gently brown the meat rolls. Using a slotted spoon, transfer, seam-side down and in one layer, to a large, shallow pan.

Combine any remaining vegetable purée and stock, check the seasoning, and pour over the meat rolls. Simmer gently for about 30 minutes, or until the meat is tender. Add a little water if needed as they cook. The sauce should be fairly thick.

Lift out the *involtini*, remove the string, and serve them with some sauce.

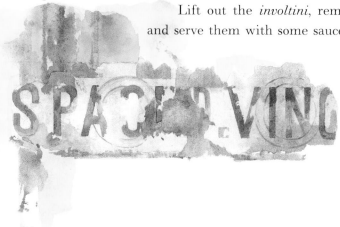

Involtini di Carne e Verza

Ground Meat Wrapped in Cabbage Leaves

There are variations of this recipe in every Roman family and trattoria, and we find it instant comfort food during the first chilly evenings towards the end of October. Traditionally it is a Jewish dish served on Simha Tora, during Succoth, or harvest time; the Jewish version omits the cheese. The cabbage leaves represent the vine leaves in the vineyards of Judea.

8 large cabbage leaves

Light stock (see page 118)

10½ ounces (298 g) ground (minced) beef, veal, or lamb

2 slices stale coarse bread, soaked in a little stock

1 small onion, finely chopped

2 tablespoons freshly grated Parmesan, or half pecorino and half Parmesan

1 tablespoon chopped fresh parsley

Salt and black pepper to taste

1 egg (optional)

Fresh tomato sauce (see page 118)

Blanch the cabbage leaves in boiling salted water for a few minutes. Lift out the leaves and plunge into ice water. Drain, arrange carefully on paper towels (kitchen paper), and pat dry. Using kitchen scissors, remove the tough central stalk, and overlap the leaf.

Heat the stock to boiling. Meanwhile, in a food processor or by hand, make a coarse paste with the meat, squeezed-out bread, onion, cheese, parsley, and seasoning. Then add the egg. Shape the meat mixture into 8 sausage shapes. Place each horizontally on a leaf, fold over the ends, then roll up the leaf so that the meat is enclosed on all sides. When all the leaves have been used, arrange the cabbage rolls in a shallow pan in one layer. Carefully pour over the boiling stock and top the meat rolls with a plate that just fits in the pan. This will prevent the leaves from unrolling during the cooking period. Simmer gently for 20 minutes. Serve on top of a little fresh tomato sauce.

DESSERTS

Most Italians like to finish their long, long meals with fresh fruit, and desserts as we know them are comparatively new. The traditional "desserts" are quite substantial, and are more like cakes, to be eaten with a fork, not a spoon. In the past they were often served with a glass of sweet wine in the afternoon to passersby. These cakes and pastries are usually bought at specialty *pasticcerie*, and every Sunday morning the city pastry shops are thronged with eager customers. Lunch guests are choosing a suitable elaborate dessert for their hostess, and the streets are full of elegant shoppers toting distinctive "designer" cake boxes. Men are engaged in their usual Sunday morning activity of buying the newspaper, downing an espresso, and choosing a cake to take home to their wives working busily at home. In summer, fruit ice creams often replace the cake at the end of lunch.

Roman restaurants are beginning to copy other countries with chocolate mousse or crème brûlée, but spoon desserts are not usually part of the home cook's repertoire.

Timballo di Ricotta

Ricotta Timbale

This is another recipe from the Roman Jewish tradition. Do not attempt to make this without very good fresh ricotta.

3 egg yolks, beaten

⅔ cup (156 g) sugar

1 pound (455 g) fresh
ricotta, drained for
1 hour

Pinch of ground
cinnamon

Grated zest of ½ lemon

3 tablespoons (44 mL)
brandy

3 egg whites, whipped to
soft peaks

Preheat the oven to 350°F (180°C/gas mark 4).

Beat the egg yolks and sugar until you have a smooth, pale cream. Stir in the drained ricotta, cinnamon, lemon zest, and brandy. Carefully fold in the beaten egg whites and spoon into an oiled baking dish. Bake for 20 minutes, then turn oven down to 300°F (150°C/gas mark 2) and bake for a final 10 minutes. Serve at once.

Fagottini di Mele

Stuffed Apples in Pastry

*I*n Rome it is difficult to find cooking apples, so I generally use the Granny Smith variety, commonly known in Rome markets as "Smit." The authentic pastry adds egg and sugar after the butter has been rubbed in, but I usually make a shortcrust pastry with the same quantities of flour and butter, using water to make the dough.

PASTRY

7 tablespoons (99 g) butter, softened

1¼ cups (200 g) all-purpose (plain) flour

Water

1 teaspoon sugar (optional)

1 small egg, beaten (optional)

———

4 cooking apples, cored

4 teaspoons quince paste or other jam (optional)

8 walnut halves, chopped (optional)

1 small egg, beaten

Sugar for dusting

To make the pastry, rub the softened butter into the flour, then add enough water to make a normal shortcrust pastry. If you want to use sugar and egg, dissolve the sugar in the egg and stir into the flour and butter, then add water as necessary. Roll into a ball, wrap in cooking foil, and leave in the refrigerator for at least 30 minutes.

Preheat the oven to 350°F (180°C/gas mark 4).

Stuff the cored apples with a little quince paste and walnuts if you like. Divide the pastry into 4 balls and roll out each to form a square. Place a stuffed apple in the middle of each square and bring the four corners to the top, using kitchen scissors to cut away the spare dough at the seams. Moisten the edges where the seams will occur and pinch together, then press flat. Using the leftover pastry, roll out and cut some leaf shapes to decorate the apples. Stick on to the top with beaten egg, brush the rest of the pastry with the egg and bake for 40 minutes. Dust with sugar and serve.

Castagne Tartufi

Chestnut Chocolate Truffles

W*hen marrons glacés are being made they frequently break, and the pieces are sold at a very good price. At Christmas I like to make these delicious truffles, which disappear very quickly.*

⅓ cup (78 mL) heavy (double) cream

3½ ounces (99 g) dark chocolate, grated

2 ounces (57 g) gianduja chocolate or other hazelnut chocolate, grated

2 ounces (57 g) pieces marrons glacés (candied chestnuts)

2 ounces (57 g) white chocolate, grated

In a double boiler over barely simmering water, heat the cream and stir in the dark chocolate and the gianduja chocolate until they melt. Remove from the heat and add the chestnut pieces, stirring well so that they are coated evenly. Place the mixture in a bowl and refrigerate for 2 hours.

Remove the bowl and quickly form the mixture into small balls. Roll these balls in the white chocolate, cover, and keep in the refrigerator until serving.

Crostata di Visciola

Sour Cherry Jam Tart

Romans have always loved the wild sour cherries used to make this tart, and in Rome it is so popular it is sometimes called crostata romana. *Traditionally, the pastry for sweet tarts is rather heavy, made with lard, sugar, and egg yolks. I prefer to make my normal short (shortcrust) pastry, but I have given both versions. I have given measures for generous servings since this tart disappears very quickly. Last time he was here my eight-year-old grandson ate half the tart at one sitting, then quietly went back for some more!*

PASTRY

2 cups (300 g) all-purpose (plain) flour

Pinch of salt

⅝ cup (149 g) butter, softened

Water

or

⅝ cup (149 g) lard

2 cups (300 g) all-purpose (plain) flour

⅔ cup (156 g) sugar

3 egg yolks, beaten

Water

Grated zest of 1 lemon

———

1 cup plus 2 tablespoons (255 g) sour cherry jam

If using the first group of ingredients to make the pastry, combine flour and salt.

Rub the butter or lard into the flour (or flour and salt mixture), then add enough water to make a normal shortcrust pastry. If you want to use sugar and egg, dissolve the sugar in the egg and stir into the flour and lard, then add water as necessary. Roll into a ball, wrap in cooking foil, and leave in the refrigerator for at least 30 minutes.

Preheat the oven to 350°F (180°C/gas mark 4).

Roll the pastry out thinly and line a 9-inch (23 cm) tart tin. Spread the jam evenly over the bottom. Cut the remaining pastry into thin strips and cover the tart with a crisscross, lattice pattern. If you have enough pastry left, make a thin twist to seal the edge of the tart. Bake for about 25 minutes.

Frappe
Fried Carnival Pastries

In Italy, Carnevale, *literally "farewell to meat," is the last frenzied fling before Lent and the obligatory fasting imposed in the past by the Church. Today in Rome the extravagant street romps are a thing of the past, but the tradition lingers on in colored confetti and streamers being thrown around the streets, and small children parading as Harlequin or Cinderella. Fried pastries are sold in all the bread shops, but I had never really seen their attraction until the year I was snowed in.*

About ten years ago Rome had a very severe winter and it snowed heavily for several days. The weight of the snow caused branches to fall off the umbrella pines, blocking roads and sending down electric cables and telephone lines. I was marooned at home off the Via Cassia with no electricity and therefore no water from the well. I built huge log fires, lit the candles, and got out the mineral water. My neighbors, who boast of being fifth-generation contadini, *or peasants, built a fire in the yard to melt the snow to mix the chicken feed, and proceeded to invite me to share their carnival cheer. A large black frying pan was wedged on the fire, and Anna started to fry batches of Angelina's light* frappe. *We munched happily, our breath steaming in the cold air, and we washed down the* frappe *with glasses of cloudy homemade wine. It was a carnival feast to remember.*

2¼ cups (350 g) all-purpose (plain) flour

3½ tablespoons (50 g) butter, softened

2 eggs, beaten

Pinch of salt

Pinch of sugar

Olive oil for frying

2 tablespoons (30 g) vanilla-flavored sugar

Beat together the flour, butter, eggs, salt, and sugar to make a smooth dough. Cover and leave to rest for an hour.

Roll out to a ¼-inch (5-mm) thickness. Cut the pastry into short ribbons and twist or knot, whichever form you prefer. Fry in hot oil, drain on paper towels (kitchen paper), and sprinkle with the vanilla sugar.

Fave Dolci/Fave dei Morti

Sweet "Fava Beans"

These sweets used to be made in November, the month that begins with the day commemorating the dead, I Morti. *Chrysanthemums are on sale along the roads leading to the main cemeteries at Verano and Prima Porta, and families from outside Rome travel to pay their respects at their family tombs. The dead used to be revered to such an extent that one of the most blasphemous, terrible curses is to insult someone's dead relatives with a shouted "Mortacci tua!" (Your dead are really ugly and terrible).*

Traditionally this recipe was very laborious because the almonds had to be pounded by hand in a mortar. A food processor makes the task less time-consuming.

7 tablespoons (99 g) sugar

3½ ounces (99 g) unblanched almonds

½ cup (75 g) all-purpose (plain) flour

1 teaspoon ground cinnamon

1 tablespoon (14 g) butter, softened

1 egg, beaten

Grated zest of ½ lemon

Preheat the oven to 350°F (180°C/gas mark 4).

In a food processor, process the sugar and almonds to make a coarse powder. Add in the flour, cinnamon, butter, egg, and zest. Work to make a stiff dough. Divide into oblongs the size of your little finger. Cut into small pieces and press to make a dent so that they resemble small fava beans. Line a baking sheet (baking tray) with baking parchment and arrange the beans so that they are not touching. Bake until golden brown, about 20 minutes.

Panna Cotta con Lamponi

Cooked Cream with Raspberry Sauce

Panna cotta *originated in Piedmont but recently, with fresh cream readily available, Roman restaurants have adopted it as their own. I love the combination of the rich smooth cream and the raspberries with their seeds. However, if preferred, the raspberries can be sieved or replaced with strawberries.*

½ envelope plain gelatin

2 tablespoons (30 mL)
   cold water

1¼ cup (296 mL) heavy
   (double) cream

5 tablespoons (71 g) sugar

Grated zest of 1 lemon

2 cups (227 g) fresh
   raspberries

Sprinkle the gelatin over the cold water and let it soak for several minutes. Heat the cream, 4 tablespoons (57 g) of the sugar, and zest and boil gently for 1 minute. Stir in the gelatin until dissolved. Pour the mixture into individual molds and leave for about 4 hours to set.

Leave a few whole raspberries for decoration and purée the rest with the remaining 1 tablespoon (14 g) sugar. Just before serving, unmold the creams and pour round the raspberry sauce.

Crespelle di Castagne con Mele Stregate

Chestnut Pancakes with Apple and Quince Filling

I love to make these pancakes in winter with quince paste and sharp apples. I use Strega liqueur to get the full Snow White bewitched-apple effect, but this can easily be omitted, or replaced with another liqueur.

4 apples, peeled, cored, and chopped

1 tablespoon (15 mL) water

4 tablespoons (114 g) quince paste

⅓ cup (57 g) chestnut flour

1 egg, beaten

⅓ cup (125 mL) milk, diluted with ⅓ cup (125 mL) water

2 tablespoons (28 g) butter

2 tablespoons (30 mL) Strega liqueur, heated (optional)

In a medium pan, cook the apples in 1 tablespoon (15 mL) water until soft. Stir in the quince paste.

Mix together the flour, egg, and diluted milk and allow to stand at room temperature for at least 30 minutes. Heat a griddle over high heat and melt the butter. Ladle batter onto hot griddle to make 8 pancakes. Keep the pancakes warm while you are cooking the rest. Spoon some apple mixture on each pancake and roll up. Pour the heated liqueur over the pancakes and serve.

BASICS

Fresh Tomato Sauce

1 small onion, finely
  chopped

2 pounds (907 g) ripe
  tomatoes, or 2 fourteen-
  ounce (397 g) cans
  peeled Italian plum
  tomatoes

2 tablespoons (30 mL)
  extra virgin olive oil

Salt and black pepper

2 tablespoons chopped
  fresh parsley or basil

Heat the oil and gently cook the onion until soft. Add the tomatoes and cook quickly until most of the juice has evaporated. Put through a food mill, season with salt and pepper to taste, and sprinkle with the fresh herbs.

Light Stock

This stock can be prepared in larger quantities and frozen. By adding the seasoning and herbs just before use, different flavors can be achieved with the same basic stock.

1 pound (454 g) lean veal
  or chicken and bone
  suitable for stock

1 onion

2 carrots

1 celery stick

6 whole peppercorns

Salt and pepper to taste

Fresh or dried herbs as
  desired (optional)

Put all the ingredients in a large pan and cover with cold water. Bring to a boil and simmer for 2 to 3 hours. Strain and allow to cool before skimming off any fat that has risen to the surface. Before use, adjust seasoning and add appropriate herbs as desired.

To Peel Tomatoes

Blanch tomatoes quickly in boiling water. Drop into ice water; the skins will slip off easily. To seed tomatoes, cut into segments and cut out seeds.

To Prepare Eggplant

Eggplants contain a bitter liquid that can spoil the taste of a dish, so they need to be "purged" before cooking. Slice or cube the eggplant and arrange in a single layer on a chopping board. Sprinkle over *coarse* salt and leave for 30 minutes. The board needs to be raised at one end so that the bitter liquid runs off. Fine salt should not be used as it is too easily absorbed by the eggplant. After 30 minutes rinse well in cold running water and pat dry.

To Roast Peppers

Peppers need to be roasted so that the indigestible skin can be removed. If the recipe requires the cooked peppers to be sieved this step can be omitted. Wash and dry the whole peppers then place on a hot grill, barbecue, or gas flame. Using tongs, turn them around until all the surfaces are black and blistering. Remove from the heat and place the peppers to cool in a brown paper bag. Close the bag so that the steam cannot escape. When cool, peel off the skin and remove the seeds and fibrous sinews.

To Trim Artichokes

If artichokes are to be trimmed and sliced they must be rubbed with half a lemon and placed in a large bowl of cold water and lemon juice. If this step is omitted the artichokes become discolored. Once the coarse tips and outer leaves have been removed, rub well with the lemon. Then using a very sharp knife, turn round the artichoke, paring off any inedible leaves. Usually you need to eliminate any part not pale yellow or light green. Rub frequently with the lemon half. If the artichoke needs to be cut into segments, divide into quarters and cut out the choke. Rub with lemon and place in the lemon water while going on to trim the rest. Leave in the lemon water for at least 30 minutes. Rinse well then proceed according to the recipe.

GLOSSARY

borlotti beans Large, round red- and pink-striped beans; they are available fresh in late summer, and dried the rest of the year round.

Castelluccio lentils Small, greenish-brown to blue lentils; also known as *lentilles de Puy*.

gianduja chocolate A kind of hazelnut chocolate.

Marsala wine Fortified sweet or dry wine from Sicily.

mascarpone cheese Thick, fresh creamy cheese made with cow's milk; originally made in Lombardy and Piedmont.

pancetta Pork cured with salt and pepper; similar to bacon.

pecorino cheese A sharp, salty, hard cheese made from sheep's milk, ideal for grating. There are several regional varieties; in this book, pecorino romano is meant.

pink trout Also known as salmon trout. It is called brown trout in North America.

prosciutto Salted, air-dried ham; the most famous are from Parma, but those from San Daniele are equally excellent.

rice (arborio, carnaroli, or vialone) All three are varieties of rice ideal for making risotto as they are starchier than other kinds of rice. Vialone is preferred.

semolina Finely milled durum wheat powder, used to make pasta and gnocchi.

Strega An herbed liqueur; *strega* means "witch" in Italian.

tomatoes, plum Small, oblong, firm-fleshed tomatoes, also known as Roma tomatoes.

tuna, ventresca cut A cut from the central, or belly, part of the fish.

vanilla-flavored sugar Make vanilla-flavored sugar by placing a vanilla pod in a closed container of granulated sugar: the flavor and aroma of the vanilla will subtly penetrate the sugar.

vongole verace clams Small, sweet, round clams found off the coast of Italy.

A GUIDE TO ROMAN FOOD

Restaurants

These are ordinary Roman trattorias that serve some of the dishes mentioned in this book. Fish is a "special" on Tuesdays and Fridays, and Thursday is the day for gnocchi. Each restaurant has a different day of the week for closing, so be sure to check opening times first. These places are known for their food, not the view, location, or style.

Jewish Specialties

Al Pompiere, Via S. Maria dei Calderari, 38, Tel: 686 8377.

Da Paris, Piazza San Calisto, 7, Tel: 581 5378. In Trastevere, not the ghetto.

Evangelista, Via delle Zoccolette, 11, Tel: 687 5810. Be sure to try the artichokes and the pasta *alla gricia.* (Dinner)

Sora Margherita, Piazza del Cinque Scole, 30, Tel: 686 4002. Very homely; not the place for an intimate lunch—be prepared to share a table. (Lunch)

Roman Fare

Checchino dal 1887, Via di Monte Testaccio, 30, Tel: 574 6318. Started life as a wine shop, cooking for the slaughterhouse workers. Now a smart restaurant with a superb wine list. The place to try offal or ox tail. A Roman institution.

Da Felice, Via Mastro Giorgio, 29, Tel: 574 6800. Best for lunch after a visit to the market. Go in and ask *very humbly* for a place to sit down. Eat the day's special.

Fans of the film *Caro Diario* will want to visit the **Garbatella** and the simple **Moschino.** Eat the day's specials. Tables outside in the summer.

Perilli, Via Marmorata, 39, Tel: 574 2415. One of the best *amatriciana* in town.

In San Lorenzo, once very "popolare" or plebeian, now the artists', students', and intellectuals' quarter, eat at **Pommidoro,** Piazza dei Sanniti, 44, Tel: 445 2692.

Above the Colosseum, near S. Pietro in Vincoli, you can eat good fresh vegetable antipasti and pasta at **Osteria da Nerone,** Via delle Terme di Tito, 96, Tel: 474 5207.

The island in the Tiber, the *isola tiberina*, houses the small trattoria **Sora Lella.** At the time of writing the trattoria is closed for maintenance: please call first. Via Ponte Quattro Capi, 16, Tel: 686 1601.

Specialty Shops in Rome

Bread

Gianfornaio, Piazzale Ponte Milvio, 35. Just around the corner from the good morning food market. Worth a visit for the spectacular innovations. Bread baskets for center table, plaits, and rolls made from dough colored with spinach, carrot, beetroot, etc. Come in the morning for the best choice.

Il Forno, 22 Campe de' Fiori. A minute corner shop always packed with customers in search of crisp pizza and traditional bread.

Palombi, Via Veneto, 114. Good traditional bread in what used to be the center of *la dolce vita*.

Panella, Largo Leopardi, 6/10. Very near the central Piazza Vittorio morning food market. Bread from all regions of Italy and other countries. Also sells dried herbs, spices, and grains. Great window displays at Christmas and Easter.

Panificio Arnese, Via del Politeama, 27. A Trastevere bakery using a traditional oven fueled with wood and hazelnut shells. The best crusty *pane casereccio* to be found in Rome. Many top restaurants get their bread here. Don't expect a shop window or serving counter or large choice of bread. You buy crusty loaves straight from the bread racks beside the ovens.

Fish

Antica Pescheria Galluzzi, Via Venezia, 26/28. A small treasure-house selling the best fish in Rome. Open every morning. Go early for the best choice, or the restaurateurs will beat you to it. Gianfranco is a great enthusiast and they will clean and fillet the fish or beat cuts of swordfish into thin slices that can be rolled and stuffed.

In the early evening, the quay at **Fiumicino,** the small port near Rome's busy airport, has a row of fish stalls selling the day's catch.

La Corte di John Fort, Via della Gatta, 1. Smoked salmon and other smoked fish, caviar, and frozen fresh salmon. One of the first shops to introduce Rome to smoked salmon.

At **Ostia,** around 6:00 p.m., the lorries drive up with the day's catch to **Taverna del Pesce di Fajola** in Via Tor, San Michele.

Rosa, at the corner stall in Testaccio morning food market, also has a good choice of fish.

Meat

Feroci, Via della Maddalena, 15. Near the Pantheon, suppliers to many local restaurants of very good quality meat.

Il Fiorentino, Piazza Campo de' Fiori, 17. Some of the best Italian meat in Rome, with French lamb and Angus beef.

Ranieri. Corner shop in the market square at Testaccio. Good fresh meat and prepared meats. Free range poultry and game in season can be ordered if not available.

Salumeria: Prosciutto, Salami, Cheeses, etc.

Antica Norcineria Viola, Piazza Campo de' Fiori, 43. Very traditional shop, selling lard, *guanciale,* ham and pork fat, and a selection of sausages. Do not expect innovations here.

Franchi, Via Cola di Rienzo, 200/204. A Mecca for those in search of the best. Also a good source of ready-prepared food.

Volpetti, Via Marmorata, 47. Near the Piramide and Testaccio market. One of the best salumeria in Rome. A great choice.

Wine

Altobelli, Via Furio Camillo, 10. Off the Via Appia, quite far from the center but good wines at a very good price.

Enoteca Bleve, Via S. Maria del Pianto, 9. Near the ghetto. Good choice of wines and adjoining room for light lunch with a good glass of wine.

Trimani, Via Goito, 20. Old established wine shop, with great choice of wines, regional olive oils and other gourmet specialties. There is an adjoining wine bar for light meals with a glass of good wine.

Cakes

Il Forno del Ghetto, Via del Portico d'Ottavia, 1. Traditional Jewish cakes.

La Dolce Roma, Via del Portico d'Ottavia, 20b. Mouthwatering cakes from many parts of the world.

Mondi, Via Flaminia Vecchia, 468. Near Ponte Milvio market; a great selection of cakes, ice creams, and canapes.

The sweet *cornetti* Romans enjoy for breakfast with their coffee can be bought in the early hours of the morning (and often are, by nightowls returning home from the *discoteca)* at **Vicolo del Cinque,** near Trastevere's Piazza Trilussa, or in Testaccio's **Via Volta.**

Ice Cream

The three most famous places for *gelati* are all between the Pantheon and Piazza Colonna: **Della Palma,** Via della Maddalena, 20/23; **Fiocco di Neve,** Via del Pantheon, 51; and **Giolitti,** Via Uffizi del Vicario, 40.

Street Markets

Street markets are found all over the city in every quarter. They are open every morning, Monday to Saturday.

Campo de' Fiori is the most picturesque, but prices are high and every year there are fewer stalls as the rents increase. Maria has the best choice of herbs and vegetables, and her son sells pots of herbs, pulses, and spices at the stall opposite.

Piazza Vittorio can be dangerous so don't go with showy jewelry or handbags. The prices are very good but keep your wits about you. This is also the market for exotic foodstuffs as the African population of Rome shop here.

Ponte Milvio caters to prosperous shoppers, and is a good place to find the first seasonal vegetables.

Testaccio is the most Roman of all the markets. It grew up near the old slaughterhouse, and it has an ugly charm all of it own. The people who work in the market are its greatest asset. See Rosa on the corner fish stall, and Rita, who sells beautiful fresh herbs.

Via della Croce is not a market as such, but a street of gourmet shops. Look for bread and pizza rustica at Fior Fiore.

Home Comforts

Castroni, Via Cola di Rienzo, 196, sells food from all over the world to gladden the hearts of expats, and those wishing to experiment with more exotic cuisines.

MAIL-ORDER SOURCES

The editors recommend the following mail-order sources for Italian ingredients. Call for catalogs.

Aux Delices des Bois, Inc.
14 Leonard Street
New York, NY 10013
212/334-1230

Mushrooms, sun-dried tomatoes, and other specialty foods.

D'Artagnan, Inc.
399–419 St. Paul Avenue
Jersey City, NJ 07306
800/327-8246

Game meats.

Dean and Deluca
Mail-order Department
560 Broadway
New York, NY 10012
212/431-1691
800/221-7714, ext. 223

Equipment and specialty foods.

G.B. Ratto International Grocer
821 Washington Street
Oakland, CA 94607
800/228-3515 (California)
800/325-3483

Specialty foods, including grains, flours, herbs, and spices.

Jamison Farm
171 Jamison Lane
Latrobe, PA 15650-9400
800/237-5262

Farm-raised lamb.

The Mozzarella Company
2944 Elm Street
Dallas, TX 75226
214/741-4072
800/798-2954

Cheeses, sun-dried tomatoes, and imported olive oils and balsamic vinegars.

Phipps Ranch
P.O. Box 349
Pescadero, CA 94060
415/879-0787

Beans and grains.

Todaro Brothers
555 Second Avenue
New York, NY 10016
212/679-7766

Imported cheeses and specialty foods.

Urbani Truffles and Caviar, USA
29–24 Fortieth Avenue
Long Island City, NY 11101
718/392-5050
800/281-2330

Truffles.

Vivande Porta Via
2125 Fillmore Street
San Francisco, CA 94115
415/346-4430

Specialty and imported foods; seeds for Italian vegetable varieties.

INDEX

Other illustrated titles by Diane Seed
from Ten Speed Press

The Top 100 Pasta Sauces

Illustrated by Robert Budwig

The bestselling collection of the most flavorsome and inviting pasta sauce recipes. Over 1,000,000 copies in print.

128 pages, full color, ISBN 0-89815-232-1 paper,
ISBN 0-89815-257-7 cloth

More Great Italian Pasta

Illustrated by Sarah Hocombe

Delightful illustrations accent this tour of regional Italian pasta recipes.

144 pages, full color, ISBN 0-89815-496-0 paper

The Top 100 Italian Dishes

One hundred perenially favorite dishes, pulled from the most beloved regional cuisines of Italy.

144 pages, full color, ISBN 0-89815-434-0 paper

Diane Seed's Mediterranean Dishes

Illustrated by Sarah Hocombe

A grand tour of the classic cuisines of the Mediterranean, from spicy North African cooking to simple Italian peasant food.

128 pages, full color, ISBN 0-89815-579-7 paper

Favorite Indian Food

Illustrated by Robert Budwig

A wonderful, evocatively illustrated introduction to the best of Indian food, featuring 125 recipes.

128 pages, full color, ISBN 0-89815-357-3 paper

Ten Speed Press
P.O. Box 7123 • Berkeley, CA 94707
(800) 841-BOOK